The Art of Cycling, Living, and Dying

The Art of Cycling, Living, and Dying

Moral Theology from Everyday Life

D. STEPHEN LONG

CASCADE *Books* · Eugene, Oregon

THE ART OF CYCLING, LIVING, AND DYING
Moral Theology from Everyday Life

Cascade Books
An Imprint of Wipf and Stock Publishers
199 W. 8th Ave., Suite 3
Eugene, OR 97401

www.wipfandstock.com

PAPERBACK ISBN: 978-1-6667-0715-1
HARDCOVER ISBN: 978-1-6667-0716-8
EBOOK ISBN: 978-1-6667-0717-5

Cataloguing-in-Publication data:

Names: Long, D. Stephen, 1960–, author.

Title: The art of cycling, living, and dying : moral theology from everyday life / D. Stephen Long.

Description: Eugene, OR: Cascade Books, 2021 | Includes bibliographical references.

Identifiers: ISBN 978-1-6667-0715-1 (paperback) | ISBN 978-1-6667-0716-8 (hardcover) | ISBN 978-1-6667-0717-5 (ebook)

Subjects: LCSH: Long, D. Stephen, 1960–. | Christian Ethics. | Cycling—United States—History. | Bicycles—United States.

Classification: BJ1251 .L67 2021 (paperback) | BJ1251 (ebook)

10/18/21

For Sophie and Emma

Contents

Acknowledgments

The following work incurs more debts than I can possibly repay, and that is the best form of debt there is. First, I must thank Ricka, who not only lived through these experiences with me, offering support and wisdom, but also read through the manuscript with care. I would have despaired without her love and encouragement. My parents, Wayne and Sue Long, also read the manuscript to help make sure that I got some of these stories right. They too have been a source of support and encouragement on this project and throughout my life. They have been a great grace, showing me what it would mean to live well as a son, husband, father, and grandfather. Bob Engel read the work, discussed it with me, and encouraged me not only to write it but also to heal well. His friendship has been a constant blessing. My children and their spouses, Jonathan, Rebecca, Adam, Lindsey, and Adam are a source of joy and wisdom that makes living worthwhile, as are our granddaughters Harper, Sophie, and Emma. Our time together, especially sitting around the table eating, discussing, and laughing has made me a better theologian and person. Lily's presence adds to that joy. The love I received from my siblings Diane, Jeff, and Sherrie, during many of the difficult times noted in the following story, has also been a grace. Many people prayed, encouraged, and supported me and my family during some difficult days and some of them read the work and encouraged me to publish it. I am grateful to Fritz Bauerschmidt, Dan Bell, Jason Byassee, Jaylynn Byassee, Sam Byassee, Michael Budde, Terri Budde, Bill Cavanaugh, Rodney Clapp, Charlie Collier, Charlie Curran, Stanley Hauerwas, Paula Gilbert, Willie Jennings, Joanne Brown Jennings, George Kalantzis, Elisabeth Kincaid, Brent Laytham, Therese Lysaught, Beka Miles, Debra Dean Murphy, Jim Murphy, Tracy Rowan, Joel Shuman, Maureen Sweeny, Cynthia Nielsen, Will Nielsen, and KK and

Kung Siu Yeo. Craig Hill, Priscilla Pope-Levison, and Jack Levison wrote me shortly after my first hospitalization, asking how I was doing. Corresponding with them about my situation was therapeutic and prompted me to put my reflections in writing, contributing to this work. I remain grateful for their concern and correspondence. The support of the faculty, staff, and graduate students at Perkins School of Theology and the Graduate Program in Religious Studies at Southern Methodist University made me glad to be a member of such a supportive community. I am also grateful for the pastors and churches that have continually prayed for us, especially the Rev. Lindsey Long Joyce and the United Church of Rogers Park, the Rev. Gary Manning and Trinity Episcopal Church, and the Rev. Susan Gorham Robb and Cox Chapel. Their prayers, meals, and notes of encouragement meant much to us. To everyone with whom I have bicycled over the years, and especially the Tosaspokesmen and Mirage Cycling—thank you. Brian Clark read the manuscript with care, making it much better in form and content. I am in his debt.

I don't recall when I first met John Wipf and Jon Stock, but I knew they were forces to be reckoned with. It was before their combined efforts made its significant contribution to theological publication. I have watched with joy as they turned a bookstore into one of the most potent publishing arms available to scholars at all levels. I have visited in Jon Stock's home and he in mine. We know each other's histories. In fact, I have visited with the community in Eugene, Oregon of which he was a part on several occasions. They know me well enough that they provided me an opportunity to ride a bicycle through beautiful Oregon. It is most fitting that this work is published by my friends at Wipf and Stock. I'm grateful.

Introduction

Surprise. Shock. Confusion. The challenges elicited by the year 2020 brought these feelings and more. The pandemic challenged us at a biological level; a small virus ended many lives and seriously harmed others. It was exacerbated at the political level by the many crises that emerged daily with yet another invocation of "unprecedented." Would democratic institutions hold? Had they come to an end? Why had medical science become so contested, the simple request to wear a mask and social distance a call to arms? Then there was the, unfortunately, all-too-familiar cultural crisis as America's racial caste system raised its ugly face repeatedly. A broad coalition of people took to the streets providing for a brief moment the hope that white supremacy might be acknowledged, challenged, and the call for Black lives to matter realized. It was a moment, sadly, too quickly eclipsed by reactionary forces. On top of these crises, I suffered my own personal one when at the age of sixty, which seemed to still be in the middle of life, I was confronted with my own mortality. Crisis piled upon crisis, coupled with month after month of quarantine, provoked much reflection. The book you hold in your hands resulted, in large part, from those reflections.

Let me be clear; quarantine was far from miserable for me. We had gathered in Chicago as a family, with my daughters and their husbands, to celebrate our granddaughter Harper's second birthday. While we were together, the shutdowns due to the pandemic began. Our places of employment went virtual, and Chicago declared a city-wide lockdown. We decided to travel north to our home in Milwaukee to support each other for the time being, unsure what the lockdown would mean or how long it would last. Collectively, we tended to my two-year-old granddaughter, Harper, made weekly trips to the grocery store, took turns cooking and cleaning, and spent the evenings helping with Harper's bath, reading stories, playing games, discussing faith and politics, and watching movies. Our daughters Lindsey and Rebecca were pregnant throughout quarantine. Becky had Sophie in May. Becky was several weeks past her due date and went to the hospital early to be induced. I assumed it would take some time for Sophie to be delivered. I went for a short bicycle ride close to home as I awaited the birth of my second granddaughter and told the family to text me the minute they heard any news. I ride with a Garmin, a small bicycle computer mounted on the handlebars that gives you information on how fast, how far, and how long you are riding. It connects to a smart phone. When anyone texts, the message appears on the Garmin. Three beautiful words flashed on the screen: "Sophie is here!" I flew home to rejoice with everyone as we waited for Becky and Adam to bring Sophie home, into our lives and into quarantine.

Then came Emma in late July. When we gathered in March we had no idea that we would be together for more than three months; in mid-summer our daughters and sons-in-laws returned to their respective homes in Chicago and Milwaukee as we waited for Lindsey to give birth to her second daughter, Emma, Harper's younger sister. We gathered once again as a family in Chicago as the due date approached. Emma came right on time. Because of COVID restrictions, we were unable to visit her in the hospital, and instead waited for her to return from the hospital with her parents, Lindsey and Adam. In the midst of a pandemic, protests, and political upheaval, our second and third granddaughters entered the world.

During quarantine, Harper found an album with pictures taken from my parents' cabin at Lake Shafer in central Indiana. She became obsessed with it, asking for it each night right before bedtime and looking at it repeatedly. We promised her a trip to the lake, and the next month, in mid-August, we gathered once more as a family at my parents' cabin. Harper and Emma's other grandparents, Chris and Lori, who are close friends, joined us, as we celebrated a fitting end to months of living closely together. Our time of quarantining together came to its completion. Ricka, my wife, returned to Chicago with Lindsey and Adam to help with Harper and Emma. Adam, Becky, and Sophie returned to Milwaukee. I drove back to Dallas to begin the fall semester and teach my undergraduate course on Christian theology at Southern Methodist University.

Our collective quarantine came to an end, but things were not back to normal. The biological, political, and cultural crises had disoriented everyday life. What we thought was normal had been upended. No one knew, nor knows, how much of it might have come to an end. What will life be like once the pandemic subsides? Will the political upheaval come to a peaceful resolution with freedom and democracy still intact? Will the ongoing power of white supremacy be named, challenged, and dismantled, or will it continue to fester and gain power? It was a difficult time, but I was proud how our family pulled together to make the best of a troubled year, a year that in the middle of multiple crises also prompted new beginnings, especially Sophie and Emma. In the midst of so many endings, we had tangible, bodily presences of new beginnings. It was hopeful. Yet, little did I know how abnormal life would become, that my own possible ending lurked around the corner.

What follows are my reflections on living and dying, on beginnings and endings, prompted by the personal crisis I experienced in October 2020. I did not see it coming; nor was I prepared for it. It was associated with my forty years of long-distance cycling, something that had become a part of my identity. The first chapter tells the story of what came to an end that fateful October morning. Endings can only occur from a beginning; in order to understand the ending well, the beginning needs to be known. For this reason, chapter 1, "Endings," is followed by chapter 2, "Beginnings." It narrates several beginnings: the invention and subsequent history of the bicycle; the beginning of my identity as a long-distance athlete; life in rural Indiana and what that history brings with it; the origins of my extended family history; the beginning of my surprising vocation as a scholar; and beginnings of friendships, parenthood, grandparenthood.

We are seldom present at the beginning, or at least insufficiently present such that we realize we are at a beginning. If we were not told stories of our birth, how would we know of our own beginning? We are already in the middle of life when we learn to make sense of its beginning and subsequent history. We take up practices that become ways of life over time that we never would have known at the beginning would be so central to our life. How was I to know that a desire to play high school basketball would culminate in years of cycling? We only have endings because of our beginnings, but we would not know either if it were not for the fact that we are always in the middle of life. When it comes to its end, we no longer know it. We are in the middle right up to that moment, and the middle is seldom whole; it comes to us broken, bringing with it fractures that are bodily, familial, cultural, ecclesial, and political. Chapter 3 examines the broken middle; making sense of the brokenness of the middle can give our life wholeness. As long as we are breathing, speaking, writing, thinking, we are in the middle, and the possibility of wholeness remains. It can give us hope. Chapter 4 traces life in the middle, looking for the virtues that can make a life worth living. The middle is oriented to the end; an end that can be mere finality. Things just stop. "It is finished." Or an end can be purposive; the end makes the middle meaningful. "It is accomplished." Chapter 5 examines these two possibilities, siding with the second.

These five chapters weave together stories of cycling, the history of my family, friendships, and diverse forms of education, with ethical and theological reflection. I have taught ethics for three decades and am convinced that the best way to teach it is not by giving people grand ethical theories but by inviting them into stories, memoirs, novels, biographies, or films. We learn ethics sitting around kitchen tables and listening to stories; participating in sports; becoming fathers, mothers, sons, daughters, grandparents, spouses; gaining practical wisdom by playing a musical instrument, acting, fishing, or riding a bicycle; taking on the role of students seeking knowledge and learning to deliberate about truth and goodness; discovering faith through regular worship; and entering into friendships. I could go on but suffice it to say ethics is mediated to us through everyday life; being attentive to it is the best teacher and the reason for the subtitle of this work. Cycling for the past forty years has taught me a great deal, formed me in virtues and vices. It required me to confront brokenness, even death, and in so doing helped me reflect on what makes a life worth living. The art of cycling is a metaphor for the practice of living well, and that includes learning how to die well—something easy to do in theory but deeply difficult to accept in practice. Perhaps it is proper that we resist it in practice, for as surprising, shocking, and confusing as life can be, it is also good, filled with joy, wonder, delight, and when done well, with faith, hope, and love that makes us want to say about each day, "Let's do it again."

1

Endings

―――――

Life drastically changed on Sunday morning October 11, 2020. The previous
day was spent like most Saturdays for the past decade or more, riding my
bicycle fifty to one hundred miles. I would leave early in the morning, sometimes by myself, sometimes with others, and return in sufficient time to
spend the afternoon with my wife, Ricka. She is central to this story, as she
is to my life. I have been an avid long-distance athlete, running or cycling,
since I was thirteen years old. Due to incessant injuries, I gave up running
in my early fifties and limited myself to cycling. For years, Saturday morning
was set aside for my longest ride of the week. Friends and family knew this
and seldom interfered with my ritual. Those hours were dedicated to time
in the saddle.

THE HABITS OF CYCLING

Time on the bicycle is enjoyable, less workout than restoration. As a scholar
and professor, my days are often spent with dead people; I read works by
deceased authors, consider their arguments, and like all scholars, seek to
advance what is good in their thought in convincing ways and leave behind
what should be left behind. Whether teaching or researching, I'm thinking,
lost in concepts, analysis, synthesis, weighing arguments back and forth,

and then doing it again. The product of your work is always unfinished. Unlike mowing grass, planting a field, or riding a bicycle, you seldom reach the point where you can say, "My work is done." Even when you publish a book, and someone bothers to read and review it, you realize that no one has the last word. More needs to be considered, read, thought, written. Authors are always in the middle of a conversation, one that existed before them and will exist after they disappear. By contrast, my daily bike ride gave me a defined sense of accomplishment. It had a clear beginning, a middle, and an end.

Cycling also gave me a way to inhabit my life as a scholar in continuity with the person I had been growing up in rural Indiana, where athletics was an inevitable, and even necessary, endeavor. An inability to be athletic, especially to play basketball, was a liability; lacking a life of scholarly pursuits was no liability. Being too bookish was viewed by many as presumptuous, elitist, or impractical. Physical endeavors mattered more than intellectual ones. Training for long-distance sports connected me to the physicality of those Indiana roots even as I lived my life among the hallowed, lofty, spires of academe.

Cycling also got me out of my study to remind me that I am a body. On research days, I had a regular routine that consisted of reading in the early morning, riding late morning or early afternoon, and writing the remainder of the day. On days I was teaching, I would ride early in the morning, leaving the house at 5:30 a.m. and riding while watching the sun rise, more prayer than exercise. The rhythmic cadence of cycling was intoxicating and, in an odd sort of way, relaxing. Cycling is not only physical; it also focuses the mind. Spinning through space at twenty mph on two wheels makes you acutely aware of your surroundings. What is that car going to do? Will that child dart into the road? Why is that dog not on a leash? Will it obey its master? Every cyclist has unexpected encounters with animals. In my case, I met rabbits, squirrels, dogs, coyotes, armadillos, ground hogs, possum, and deer. And once, in Oregon, a black bear, darted across the road or path in front of me while I was cycling. The unexpected intensifies attention, freeing the mind from unnecessary distraction in order to focus intently on matters at hand. Riding in a group known as a peloton within a few inches of other cyclists before and behind you, to your left or right, is thrilling; all your senses are on full alert in an effort to anticipate the inevitable lapse in judgment some other cyclist might make, resulting in catastrophic consequences. You become absorbed in the moment.

My habit was to ride thirty miles Monday through Friday with a longer ride on Saturday, at least while the weather was good, and on Sunday rest. I began cycling at the age of twenty. Recovering from back surgery, I purchased a bicycle and rehabbed by riding from the residential boys' home where I was working to the university I attended and back. It happened to be a thirty mile round trip and that distance was roughly equivalent to the eight to thirteen miles I previously ran daily. The thirty miles stuck, and I more or less did it for the next forty years. In some years it was impossible to ride: one year spent working in a juvenile delinquent center, another in Honduras; the first few demanding years of graduate school and parenthood also took their toll on my time cycling. Prior to turning fifty, I would run or play basketball in the winter, not being a fan of winter cycling. Two things occurred in my fifties that made me a year-round cyclist, even in Wisconsin's frigid winters. First was the inevitable losses that come with age. I could no longer run or play basketball. It was cycling or nothing. I could, of course, ride indoors and I often did, but riding a bicycle indoors was like going to the beach in a hazmat suit. It defeated a main reason to ride, to enjoy being outside. Second, I began to ride with a new cycling club, the Tosaspokesmen, or Spokesmen, whose motto is "All weather is good weather." The guys who rode year-round would supplement this motto by saying, "There is no bad weather, only bad clothing." Following their lead, I began to ride year-round as well. They introduced me to studded snow tires and the joy of winter riding through snow, ice, and cold. Granted, we would ride fewer miles at diminished speeds in Wisconsin's frigid temperatures.

For the first thirty years of cycling, I never kept track of my mileage. The only means to do so were charts filled in by pencil and that was too much work. Cell phones and apps like Map My Ride and Strava changed that, making it easy to track mileage with the press of a button. Strava is Facebook for cyclists. Linked to a Garmin or smart phone, the statistics for the day's ride are uploaded and cyclists near and far can give you kudos and comment on your ride. Initially resisting, skeptical of the fascination with recording every ride and comparing it with others, I too eventually succumbed, joining Strava in 2013, and then purchasing a Garmin that kept track of myriad cycling statistics. It was addicting, monitoring speed, distance, elevation, exertion, heart rate, and comparing your accomplishments with your own previous rides and other cyclists. In 2015 the Spokesmen set forth a challenge: who could be the first to ride 10,000 miles that year? I am not fast, but I have endurance. The challenge played to my strength; I took it up. I was not the first, my friend Jeremy was, but I did manage to ride 10,773 miles that year and many of them with him, and with my friend Kurt, who worked with me at Marquette University. The Spokesmen celebrated our accomplishment with a keg and introduction into an unofficial "10,000-mile club."

The Spokesmen celebration of the 10,000 mile club in 2015: Stephen (right)
with Jeremy and Kurt.

Spending so much time on the bike in 2015 prompted me to reflect
on cycling. Reading about it and discussing it with others, I began writing
the early stages that became this book. The following year I moved from
Wauwatosa, Wisconsin to Dallas, Texas and became the Cary M. Maguire
University Professor of Ethics at Southern Methodist University. Ricka
and I kept our home in Wisconsin because our daughters, sons-in-law and
grandchildren live in Chicago and Milwaukee. Our son was in Los Angeles.
We would return to Wisconsin December through January and summers.
Cycling in Texas was easier from September through May. Cycling in Wisconsin was easier from May through September. It was the best of both
worlds. I rode with the Spokesmen in Wisconsin and Mirage Cycling in
Dallas, making good friends in both places. I had more time for cycling
in my fifties than I did the previous two decades with their demands from
parenting, graduate school, and the pressures of teaching, researching, and
writing. I was in the best shape of my life.

AFFAIRS OF THE HEART

After completing more than 10,000 miles at the age of fifty-five, I set a goal of riding 10,000 miles each year until I turned sixty. Despite periodic crashes, illness, and professional and family obligations that kept me off the bike, I achieved that goal. Then I turned sixty and wondered what next. I set a goal of 12,000 miles for 2020, a new potential personal mileage record at the age of sixty. That requires riding an average of 27.4 miles each day or 192 miles per week. I normally took Sundays off, so I needed to average 33 miles per day. I was 500 miles ahead of schedule on October 10, 2020 when life drastically changed.

The weather was splendid that Saturday morning, cool for Texas with little wind. I tried to ride at least one century (100 miles) each month, and this day was perfect for it. I made my usual preparations—a large breakfast, two cups of coffee—then selected my most comfortable long-distance kit (a kit is a cycling outfit consisting of shorts with straps that hold them up and a matching jersey), rubbed chamois butter on the padded chamois of my cycling shorts to keep from chafing, filled my water bottles with hydration mix, and packed chews and gels for quick energy in the pockets of my jersey. Because the Coronavirus pandemic was still raging, I placed a mask in my back pocket, in case I needed to stop at a convenience store.

I had not been riding much with others during the pandemic, but because I intended to ride a century that day I planned a route that would begin with fifteen solo miles to the start of the Mirage Cycling club's Saturday morning ride, known as the South Loop. Nearly every serious cyclist in Dallas knows this route and rides it on the weekends. It is a fifty-mile route that includes several hills. Elk hill was always challenging for me. It is short but steep and comes around the thirty-fifth mile of the South Loop. The strongest cyclists hit it hard and then continue to push the pace once the peloton crests the hill; hang on during that hard exertion or have the dispiriting experience of watching the peloton ride away while you are now committed to riding the last fifteen miles of the South Loop alone, or perhaps with the others who had been dropped.

I felt particularly strong as we arrived at Elk Hill on my fiftieth mile for the day. I picked out my friend Phillip's wheel, knowing he would stay with the peloton and with effort I should be able to stay with him. The peloton began its serious exertion. A few cyclists fell off the back. Determined to hold Philip's wheel, I rode up and over the hill and through the exertion that continued once we crested it. My heart rate elevated, making breathing difficult but it soon relaxed as we pushed along the straightaway. I set a new personal record on Elk hill that day. I had ridden it forty-eight times and this was the fastest yet. Out of breath but clinging to the peloton, I took a certain pride on being one of the oldest cyclists who could still hang on.

It was a beautiful day in the saddle. I felt strong and relaxed and set several personal records, riding the South Loop with an average speed of 23.4 mph. I had thirty-five more miles to ride to complete the century and I rode them alone. Riding with others in a peloton is much more efficient than riding by yourself. Other than when you ride at the front and pull the peloton along behind you, you are putting forth significantly less energy while drafting behind others than riding by yourself. I had even taken one pull at the front that day during the South Loop, and I still felt fresh as I finished my century alone. I arrived home before noon, having averaged 20.3 mph for the 100 miles. Anytime I can still average more than 20 mph for a long ride, I am satisfied. I took it as a sign of my good health and fit condition. I told my wife how satisfied I was with the day's ride. She knew it was rather silly for a sixty-year-old man to be concerned about such trivial matters, but she supported my cycling addiction that day just as she had for the thirty-six years of our marriage. She never knew me when I wasn't cycling. We had a running joke that I was allowed to discuss cycling for fifteen minutes each day and then we had to discuss something more substantive. She even tolerated watching hours on end of the great cycling tours—Tour de France, Giro d'Italia, La Vuelta a España. I would turn on the television in the morning, mute the sound, and read while periodically observing the race. She would come in, see it on the television, and ask, "How can you watch this? They were riding bicycles hours ago and they are still just riding bicycles."

After I told her how well I had ridden that Saturday, she congratulated me, and not in a condescending tone. She could care less how fast I rode a bike, but she knew it mattered to me and for that reason normally inquired about my ride once it was completed. She headed out the door to enjoy some sun and I began my warm down, stretching and rolling out my not-so-young muscles. At my age, post-ride stretching was essential to avoid injuries. As my heart rate slowed I felt light-headed and sat down. It was not an unfamiliar feeling, often accompanying the cool down after strenuous exertions as my heart rate slowed to its normal rate. Yet in the past month, something seemed to have changed. Two months previous I had a ringing in my ears, became light-headed, and the room closed in around me; it faded to dark as my breathing became labored. I consciously slowed my breathing, focused on seeing, and the light returned. It was scary so I told Ricka what had happened. I trusted her with medical matters.

Ricka worked as an oncology nurse manager at the hospital for years, often taking care of young people with terminal illness. Her vocation was to assist many patients as best she could so that they might be well enough to die at home. She honored my vocation as a professor of theology and ethics, but once asked, "If I make a mistake, people die. If you make a mistake, what happens?" I most likely told her that was a question based on the discredited verificationist principle to which I did not need to provide an answer, and she most likely rolled her eyes. (The verificationist principle states that if you do not have the means to verify the truth of a proposition then the proposition lacks meaning. Because the verificationist principle itself cannot be verified on its own terms, it fell out of favor among philosophers, although it is making a return among economists of late.)

Ricka expressed concern about my episode that day and suggested we monitor it. Because of the coronavirus, I was in no hurry to see the doctor. We decided to wait and see if there were other episodes or if it was a one-off. It did not recur for the next six weeks. We are not a family who neglects medical care or refuses to take symptoms seriously, nor one who overreacts to life's aches and pains. When you spent decades, as Ricka had, tending to people in the gravest of conditions, you learn when to be alarmed and when not to be. We both recognized the importance of science and medicine. We never assumed you had to choose between faith and reason. Because science mattered to us, the first time I had an abnormal EKG we were sufficiently alarmed to seek medical counsel.

In my late thirties, I experienced fluttering in my chest. I mentioned it to Ricka and she would take my pulse, but never felt anything odd. After several occurrences, she suggested that the next time it occurred I call her at the hospital and have an EKG. One day I did, and she had a physician read my EKG. The doctor looked at it with an alarmed expression. He then looked at me and asked, "Do you feel okay?" I said, "Well, I did, but now I'm not so sure. What is going on?" "This EKG shows that you are having a myocardial infarction" (a heart attack.) I felt fine but this was worrisome. He advised a stress test, and I underwent it, the first of many. Although the EKG looked abnormal, I had no adverse symptoms. From that point on my EKG was always abnormal, showing a left bundle branch block. Every time I had an EKG, I was back on the treadmill performing a stress test.

Because of the regularity of the irregularity, I underwent a battery of tests over the years. First, I kept a halter monitor on for several weeks. Then I had a dye injected in my heart to make sure it was pumping correctly. It was followed by several stress tests. Finally, a cardiac electrophysiologist put the electrical currents in my heart through extensive testing, including one test that took place in the ER because failing the test resulted in the heart stopping altogether. They explained this to me as I lay on the hospital bed. The thought ran through my mind that perhaps this was not the best idea I ever had. I already had multiple cardiac workups without any negative findings. Was I tempting fate? Yet Ricka and I wanted to be sure once and for all that everything was fine and that I was not doing permanent damage to my heart with my long-distance activities. Ricka went with me to the ER and then to work in the same hospital where I had my procedure. She spent the next hour waiting to hear those words that make everyone in the hospital scramble, "Code blue, code blue." Fortunately, those words never came. The cardiac electrophysiologist diagnosed my irregular EKG as an asymptomatic Brugada EKG. Since the symptom of the syndrome is sudden death, being diagnosed as asymptomatic was reassuring. He encouraged me to get regular checkups, and then said the words that nearly a quarter of a century later may very well have saved my life. "If you ever black out, you will need to get medical attention immediately. Worst-case scenario, you might need a pacemaker."

Between those cardiac workups and October 11, 2020, I had shoulder surgery, two back surgeries, and a gall bladder removed. Each time I would not be cleared for surgery because of the abnormal EKG and found myself back on a treadmill despite my plea with the surgeon that my abnormality was my normality. I had no recurring problems except for the occasional light-headedness and spells with labored breathing walking upstairs or cycling up steep hills. I chalked them up to my low heart rate. In 2013, I had an episode cycling up hill. All of a sudden I could not breathe, inducing panic. Confused at being unable to do something I regularly did, I stopped, took off my helmet, and rested. It passed and I completed the ride.

I made an appointment with my physician, wondering if I had exercise-induced asthma or something that was hindering my breathing. She was worried about my heart and so once again I found myself performing a stress test. The EKG was hooked up, and I began walking then running while the treadmill inclined. The imaging agent Tetrofosmin was injected into my heart and I was watching my heart and the EKG with the technician when all of a sudden the EKG went wild. The technician stopped the treadmill and asked me to lie down, inquiring as to how I felt. I felt fine. The records from that study state, "With the patient at maximum tolerated treadmill stress, . . . Tetrofosmin was injected IV and Spect myocardial perfusion imaging begun within 60 minutes. The patient reached 92% of predicted maximum heart rate. The patient stopped because of EKG changes." I was confused by the EKG changes and questioned the cardiologist, who thought they most likely resulted from my heart's thick muscle and low rate. Because the changes were unaccompanied by any symptoms, he cleared me for my ongoing activities but encouraged me to follow up every other year. Then I moved in 2015.

FLAT LINES AND ARTIFICIAL BEATS

Seven years after that last cardiac workup on Sunday morning, the day after I had the successful 100-mile ride, I went about my Sunday routine, looking forward to a day of rest. I was drinking a second cup of coffee, reading a biography of the political philosopher John Rawls, when that odd feeling from the previous day and month overcame me for the third time. My first thought was, "I must be tired." I had not slept well the night before. As the buzzing in my ears intensified, the room narrowed and began to fade, I thought I knew what to do. Breathe slow and intentional, focus attention, and then . . .

A frightening, primal groan brought me out of the darkness that had enveloped me. It took a few moments for me to realize that my body was making that noise. An instinctual desire to live set in, my body gasped for breath, bringing me back to consciousness. Dazed, I had no idea where I was, what time of day it was, or how long I had been unconscious. I slowly came out of it but remained confused. I could not figure out why Ricka had not heard my groaning and come to my aid. I thought it was the night before and she was still in her chair sitting next to mine. I looked over and did not see her. She had recently returned to Dallas from Chicago after assisting our daughter with Harper and Emma. I could not remember if she was in Chicago or with me in Dallas. Gradually, light began to dawn, and I realized it was morning.

I stumbled into the bedroom looking for her, found her still sleeping and yelled, "Ricka!, Ricka!," then walked back into the living room, collapsing on the couch, trying to make sense of what just happened. It was as if some sinister force rose up and snatched my thought, vision, speech, hearing, and ability to move, trying to keep them from me and I was struggling to recover them. She could see I was in distress. I was pale and sweaty. She took my pulse, and noted it was forty and irregular. "We need to get to the hospital." I agreed, but I wanted to do some research to figure out which hospital would be best for what with increasingly clarity we both acknowledged was a significant cardiac event. Despite all our precautions, the day had arrived when the cardiac irregularities bore their fruit. I did not have a primary physician or cardiologist in Dallas, something I now know was a mistake. I had a false sense that because I was in such good physical condition, could still ride my bicycle as long and fast as I did, and had previously been proactive in cardiac care, that I would be fine.

I worried about showing up unexpected at an unfamiliar hospital. I knew I needed to see someone, but perhaps it would be better to do it on my own terms. I had colleagues who would know the best cardiologists in Dallas. I should consult them. I was also scheduled to teach a Sunday school class on theology and economics that morning and was looking forward to it. Besides, Sunday was a much longed-for day of rest. Who wanted to spend it at the ER? Ricka insisted that we go immediately. She reminded me what the cardiologist said decades ago, "Look, worst-case scenario, you will need a pacemaker." Neither of us thought that would actually happen, or at least not immediately. Neither of us knew how much distress my heart was in. But I knew Ricka's wisdom on medical matters, and I was not recovering as quickly as I desired, so I agreed. We decided to go to the closest hospital, City Hospital at White Rock Lake. White Rock Lake was my favorite place to bicycle, riding there nearly every Monday through Friday, passing by City Hospital and barely noticing its existence.

I also worried about going to the hospital during the pandemic, both because I did not want to contract the coronavirus and I did not want to take up unnecessary medical attention when so many were suffering. But the odd feeling had not dissipated. I remained weak and my heart was acting strange. The buzzing in my ears and contracting vision repeatedly occurred as I tried to push them away. I walked into the ER and told the attending nurse what had happened and that my wife insisted on bringing me to the ER. "Why did I say that?" I wondered as the words came out of my mouth. I too knew that I needed to be here. Did I think going to the ER was a sign of weakness? What foolishness. The nurse took my vitals and began an EKG. I told him that the EKG would be abnormal. He looked at it and asked, "I don't think it should be this abnormal." I also told him that I have a low heartbeat, usually between fifty and sixty beats per minute. He showed me that it was forty-five and decreasing. "Your vital signs are very concerning," he said. "I think it is good that your wife insisted you come to the ER."

They admitted me and hooked me up to a heart monitor that blurted out a warning signal when a heart rate became dangerously low. It now beeped continuously as my heart rate consistently dipped below forty bpm. The nurse informed us that she could not set the warning on the machine lower than forty and apologized for the constant alarm. They also placed paddles on my chest in case they needed to resuscitate me. That was a bit alarming, but the severity of my situation had not yet sunk in. It was happening too fast. I brought several books with me to the hospital and began to read one; Ricka sat nearby doing a crossword puzzle. The warning from the monitor was constant and annoying, but I did not seem to be crashing so the ER nurse stopped coming in to check when the warning went off. Ricka watched the monitor and asked how I felt. I was fine when my heartbeat was in the low forties but when it dipped below thirty-eight, the buzzing, light-headedness, and darkness began to return. The episodes became more regular now, and Ricka noticed the correlation between the episodes and my lowering heartbeat. The monitor was regularly sending out its warning signal and no one was coming because it did not correlate with my heart crashing. Until it did.

I don't recall what happened next. I was trying to calm myself and read as we waited on a physician when Ricka said my heart rate fell below thirty and then the EKG went flat. The darkness overtook me once again and the same primal groaning woke me. When I came to, Ricka was running in with the ER nurse, who was followed by several others. Ricka said I never closed my eyes but just started groaning and reaching out for her. I have no memory of that, only the horrifying memory of being enveloped in darkness and suffocation that slowly gave way to light and labored breathing. For ten seconds my heart stopped; the EKG indicated a complete blockage. The electrical circuit that was supposed to stimulate my ventricles to pump blood throughout my body ceased to work. When I looked at Ricka's face, it hit me for the first time that I was in serious condition. She looked alarmed and that seldom happened. The physician was now with us, letting us know that the cardiologist had been informed of an emergency. For the first time I thought to myself, "You might die today." I didn't think that was really possible, but the alarms around me were unnerving. Death still seemed more like a theoretical than a practical possibility. After all, I had ridden 100 miles just the day before, setting several personal records. I was healthy and fit. People like me don't die of heart failure.

I now knew what had happened earlier that morning. My heart had shut down twice that day and in between it had never fully recovered. I did not want to experience a third time, nor did I have any clue what that might mean for my weakening body. I then had this strange conversation with myself, trying to convince myself that I should take seriously what was occurring. "Well, what should you do on a day you might die?" First, pray. I said the Lord's Prayer and several others I knew by heart (pun intended). Second, tell the people you love that you love them. This second thing was trickier. It was early Sunday morning, and I did not want to alarm anyone unnecessarily. Such a phone call would surely cause concern and I thought my chances of making it through this were better than the alternative, but I was uncertain and so I decided to call our children. Our two daughters answered right away, and I told them that I was headed for an emergency pacemaker and that I wanted them to know I loved them. Our oldest granddaughter got on the phone and told me she loved me too. I was unable to get hold of our son in Los Angeles; I asked Ricka to call him as soon as possible and tell him as well. Then I called my parents and told them the same. I could tell that they were shocked and worried.

Within two hours, the cardiologist had arrived, I had been prepped for surgery, a wire inserted through my right groin into my heart and hooked up to an external battery. It all happened so quickly that I had no time to think about it or ask questions. I did not even realize that they had put the versed-fentanyl into my IV as they began threading the wire into my heart. I was relaxed and wondered why I was not feeling any of this. The cardiologist explained what was going on and questioned me as he worked. "What do you do for a living?" I had been working on a manuscript for several years entitled *On Learning and Teaching Ethics* that began with how often I receive this question in diverse settings and how it causes some trepidation to answer. I answered that I teach moral theology, a discipline that goes back to the Middle Ages and brings theology and ethics together. If I emphasize the theological aspect of the discipline, I often get awkward questions about religion. People seem more divided today on whether teaching theology is something good or bad than they do ethics. Tell someone that you teach theology and you are likely to encounter some opposition. Those who favor its teaching can, on occasion, be just as alarming, given what they think theology should be and what theologians should do.

If I answer that I teach ethics, people generally think that I'm doing something good but follow-up questions on how I teach ethics generate confusion. Perhaps it was the fentanyl, but I lacked any inhibition in telling the cardiologist that I teach theology and ethics. He seemed interested as he pushed a wire through my groin into my heart and asked, "What do you think about the new atheists?" I was impressed that a cardiologist knew such people existed. I told him that I prefer the old ones. He then asked me specific questions about the popular atheists Richard Dawkins and Christopher Hitchens. I explained to him how I thought they missed something that Nietzsche recognized. For them, religion could be dismissed without any significant loss. Architecture, hymns, spiritual practices could be reclaimed simply in a new scientific mode. "God" was nothing more than one more item in the universe to be affirmed or denied without much consequence. Theism or atheism mattered little for everyday life. Nietzsche at least recognized that the death of God was to be mourned before it could be celebrated, and that it changed everything. At least, that is how I remember the conversation going. As I recall, the cardiologist liked my answer. I was on a fentanyl cocktail so I might not have been as lucid as I imagined. Ricka told me that the cardiologist referred to our conversation in his post-procedure follow-up with her. At least I was not hallucinating.

And it was finished. The temporary pacemaker had been installed before I completed my (at least to my mind) impressive discourse on the old and new atheists. It had been a surreal day. My heart had stopped twice.

I had been rushed into emergency surgery and had a conversation with a cardiologist who knew about old and new atheism while he placed a wire in my heart, taped it to the side of my leg, and connected it to a battery hanging at the top of my hospital bed. The first heart failure happened at 6 AM and the second at 10 AM; it was now around noon. In only slightly more than the time it had taken me to ride the century the previous day, which began at 6:30 AM and finished at 11:40 AM, I now was hooked up to an external battery insuring that my heart kept beating. My life had changed such that a mechanical device would be a constant companion for its remainder. The adage "what a difference one day makes" played on a loop in my head.

The cardiologist's assistant then informed me what had transpired and what would happen next. "The battery connected to that wire is keeping your heart beating in case it stops again. You need to lie still at no more than a thirty-degree angle until we can get the permanent pacemaker installed. You cannot move your right leg. We will try to schedule you for surgery for the permanent pacemaker tomorrow, hopefully tomorrow morning, but it depends on the cardiologist's schedule and any emergencies that might come up. At the latest, we will schedule you for Tuesday. You will not be able to eat or drink anything after midnight until the surgery." Ricka asked the cardiologist why they did not simply put in the permanent pacemaker. He responded that my heart was too unstable for the procedure. First, the emergency pacemaker would stabilize my heart and then they would discern what type of permanent pacemaker I needed.

I was in the ICU lying motionless, miserable, grateful, confused. The sinister force that had taken sight, speech, and thought from me twice that day had now left me alone with thoughts and emotions that I could not turn off. Ricka stayed as long as she could until they finally asked her to leave because of the hospital's COVID protocol. I was grateful that they allowed her to be in the ER and ICU as long as they did. I asked her not to come back the next day until I was scheduled for surgery. I lay there alone from noon on Sunday until 5 PM on Monday when they finally scheduled the surgery. In the meantime, they set my emergency pacemaker to 80 bpm.

Given that my normal heart rate was 50 to 60 bpm, the artificial heartbeats coursing through my body were disquieting, making it impossible to sleep. Its artificiality was a vivid reminder of what occurred—boom-boom, boom-boom—there was no escape, which in one sense was good. I did not need to worry about slipping into that darkness a third time. But in another sense the artificiality was threatening: what would it mean to live depending upon something artificial to keep my heart beating? I tried to read, but to no avail. I listened to a few podcasts and lectures on my phone, but my mind could not focus, the questions raised by my heart's failure crowded them out. I called my brother Jeff and two sisters Diane and Sherrie and told them I loved them. We chatted for a time and they expressed their concerns and prayers. Then I turned to Netflix, binge watching series to make the sleepless hours pass. I calculated how many episodes I would need to watch to while away the time until surgery as I went through one of the longest nights of my life; the only one longer was when my son had attempted to take his life and Ricka and I drove through the night to retrieve him from the ER.

By the time Ricka arrived Monday afternoon, I was an unpleasant person. The psychological effect of the wire connected to the battery connected to my heart was both comic and tragic. I Facetimed with family members, showing them the battery hanging at the top of the hospital bed and said, "Look, there is my heartbeat." My dad joked that I would be okay because we had a battery charger at his lake cabin. The lack of sleep, food, and water had made me cranky. Lying in the same position for more than twenty-four hours was taking its toll. Not knowing what a permanent pacemaker would mean was disconcerting. Would it feel as awkward as this emergency one? I should be grateful to be alive, but I was so miserable that I could not muster much gratitude, and that only made me more miserable for my inability to feel gratitude. The cardiologist and others had given up their Sunday mornings to keep my heart working, but the cardiologists had been called to an emergency on Monday, meaning that meant my surgery was scheduled for later in the day than originally planned. I knew that I should be patient, but I wanted to be taken care of first. My intellect and will were at odds. Ricka's arrival on Monday afternoon helped. She could tell I was out of sorts and talked me through it, not capitulating to my self-recognized but nonetheless indulged self-centeredness and doing so with candor and love. A sudden illness easily makes one self-absorbed. It is as if you are the only one who has experienced some deep mystery about life. Then someone tells you that they, or their uncle, or child, friend, and so on went through the same thing and lived through it well, and to be honest, it generates feelings of resentment because it forces you out of that comforting self-absorption. Other people have been where you are. Your situation is not unique; it is the norm. You too grow old, your body fails, and you bear its failings. Did you think you could avoid this, put it off forever? That sinister force that takes the breath of all living beings always has the last word, or at least the next-to-last one. No one can avoid its encounter even if everyone is surprised by it and does all that they think they can to keep it at arm's length.

Eventually my new permanent pacemaker found its place and I spent one more night in the hospital. Ricka picked me up and we returned home. We drove past White Rock Lake on a beautiful, clear Tuesday morning at a time when I might have been out cycling. I observed the riders along the lake and tried to gain perspective on what had transpired the past three days, but what had taken place and its consequences were too confusing. Something had come to its conclusion, but what *it* was remained elusive. Was it three decades of worry that something might be seriously wrong with my heart? Was it a sense of being healthy, physically fit? Was it the ability to be the long-distance athlete I had been since the age of thirteen? Was it the end of trivial matters? Was it the loss of a facet of my identity? Was it life as I had known it before October 11, 2020? Was it life itself? No, it could not be the latter because here I was returning home with Ricka. It was too normal. I was grateful for having regained a functioning heart on this third day since it failed me, but a nagging sense of loss pressed down upon me. What it was I did not know because I did not know what lay ahead.

2

Beginnings

Everything has its beginning, except God and possibly, if Aristotle were correct, the universe. Jewish, Christian, and Islamic theologians in the Middle Ages were troubled by Aristotle's argument that the universe was eternal. Only God was eternal, and all three traditions assume that God was a free creator, which meant that creation must have a beginning because it was not divine. Beginnings identify creatures, distinguishing them from God. From persons to the environments in which they work, their family, political organizations, neighborhoods, and their cultural products, creatures begin. Language itself is a creature, beginning in time, extended through it and coming to an end. This is as true of the spoken word as it is the written.

In Christian theology, God's creating activity is not a past act, but like a grand symphony that never comes to an end, an ongoing one. In his overlooked work "On Music," St. Augustine set forth a doctrine of creation in terms of music. Every creature is like a musical note that the divine summons forth and gives its moment. When it comes to an end, its beauty lingers within the harmony that makes it more than it would be by itself. As creatures, we must learn to be like all others with our beginning, middle, and end. We too are invited to participate in the ongoing act of creation, the selfless act by which God ceaselessly donates being to all that exists, summoning it forth and giving it its moment.

WHY RIDE A BIKE? WHY WRITE
ON RIDING A BIKE?

I began work on a book on cycling five years before my cardiac incident, but something more pressing managed to sideline this project. I would periodically take it up, beginning it again, but each time didn't seem to be the right time to devote to it; a more fitting use of my time was required, one presented by my academic and ecclesial vocation. More pressing writing projects intervened: *The Perfectly, Simple Triune God*; *Augustinian and Ecclesial Christian Ethics*; and *Truth-Telling in a Post-Truth World*. Convalescing during the first week after my heart incident and reflecting on the questions that closed the last chapter prompted a reminder that I had hoped one day to write a reflection on what it meant to be a long-distance cyclist, on what it taught me, good or bad, about being human. An outpouring of prayer and support inundated my social media accounts, email, and text messages. Many of them stated something along these lines: "You are one of the fittest people I know. How could this happen to you?" I responded and explained my health situation. Putting my experience into words was therapeutic; it motivated me to return to reflect on my forty years of cycling and how it fit into my life and my inevitable, albeit thankfully deferred, death. I returned to the words I had previously written on cycling. Without much to do but rest, I loaded the manuscript on my computer and read the first sentence I had written some five years prior. The opening words now seemed prophetic: *Perhaps I cannot finish this book until I cannot. By that cryptic comment I mean this: writing on riding lacks completeness until riding ceases and I can write on my completed riding.* Something now appeared to be completed, so I decided to return to those earlier reflections. It was an opportune time to revisit it because one thing I had gained was time. I had ridden ten to fifteen hours per week for years. Unable to ride for the next several months, I returned to that earlier, incomplete work.

Retrieving and restarting the previous work on cycling helped me deal with the psychological pressures my new normal presented. Cycling had been part of my life for decades. It was there before I met Ricka, started a family, became ordained, or pursued an academic vocation. Asked why I do it, my answers vary: health, competition, environmental stewardship, vanity, sanity, camaraderie, beauty, self-discovery, athletic prowess, compensation. I commuted by bike from financial necessity; we could only afford one car. I commuted by bike from financial luxury, trying to justify owning so many bikes. Is there a coherence to those answers, something that brings them together that accounts for, gives a rendering of, all that time spent on a bicycle?

What unifies my life, any life? Now as I approach old(er) age, another question emerges—what will it mean not to cycle? What happens when my body finally fails, and how will that occur? It could happen with my will, the desire to ride disappearing. It could happen with my intellect, if I discover after all this time, cycling held forth no *reason* for me; I had deceived myself. Giving up cycling might redeem the time remaining. It could happen with my soul, since I have had moments in which I detected a voice asking me, "With all I have given you, is this worthy of your limited span? Is it responsible to the great demands on your and every other person's life? When millions are hungry, homeless, refugees, should you take the time?" Then again, it could just be my hips, back, knees, muscles, shoulders, ankles, heart, or lungs that finally fail. And there is always the possibility that a drunk, texting, or inattentive driver puts an end to my cycling, as could a darting animal or my own stupidity. However it happens, that moment of an ending will come, and I wonder if it will bring insight, an answer to the question whether I lived a life worthwhile or squandered so much that was given to me. Cycling forces the question; it isolates, quiets, and compels attention. It demands focused attention to the quotidian, to the little everyday things that one might otherwise miss.

Early Saturday morning in the winter of 2013 I was riding my bicycle with the Spokesmen on a cold twenty-degree day. The cold did not stop us from mounting our bikes and heading out on our regular Saturday-morning roll, riding on a frigid Milwaukee morning, braving the elements. We had a rule that we only rode as many miles as the temperature. We settled on a brief twenty-mile ride to Lake Michigan and back to the village of Wauwatosa where we began. Riding toward Lake Michigan, which would surely be colder, was not the smartest thing we ever did, but there we were. I was taking my turn at the head of the peloton, the formation, I have noted, that lets cyclists ride more efficiently. Riders ride in a line, taking turns at the front blocking the wind, and then with a flip of the elbow a rider will signal they are finished and peel off to take their place at the back of the pack, recuperating until they arrive at the front again.

Riding in a peloton is a form of art; the diverse colors of bikes and kits, the whir of chains, the finesse of bodily movements, the rhythmic breathing, streaming though urban or rural landscapes—it is all pure beauty. Cyclists will use at least twenty percent less energy drafting behind a rider rather than riding at the front, especially into the wind. The winds coming off Lake Michigan can be strong and cold. Bundled up in my cycling gear, riding in the front against the wind, I was lost in the rhythmic silence of the whirring cadence, chains recycling through their rings propelling the wheels; the noise punctuated with consistent breathing when all of a sudden a car pulled up beside me and a young man, apparently on his way to work, rolled down his window and shouted, "Hey, why are you guys out riding?" He must have thought we had a purpose in what we were doing, some reason for riding such as preparing for some race, raising money for charity, trying to get to a special destination. His question interrupted the rhythmic cadence and caught me up short. I did not have an answer, or at least not one I could shout from the edge of the road into a car window to a passing motorist. He slowed traffic to our pace as he waited for an answer; I felt obligated to say something. So I shouted, "Just for fun." He looked at me incredulous, rolled up his window, accelerated to the proper speed for the flow of automobile traffic, and disappeared, visibly disappointed in my answer. He seemed to be shaking his head as if to say, "Why would anyone be out riding for no reason in this weather?"

His question stayed with the small band of cyclists riding on that cold winter morning. "What did that motorist say to you," a fellow rider asked after our ride once we were drinking coffee in a warm coffee shop, another crucial element in our Saturday cycling ritual. "He asked why we were riding." "What did you tell him?" "Just for fun." The ridiculousness of my answer caused a great deal of laughter as others chimed in. "You should have told him we ride in this weather because we are manly men." "Or tell him we are idiots." After our ride, we cyclists, men in their thirties, forties, and fifties clad in brightly colored Lycra continued the conversation that the friendly motorist initiated. Why do we ride, apparently going nowhere?

IN THE BEGINNING WAS THE BIKE

Ride a bicycle and the world not only looks but also is different. Bicycling creates a world, bringing forth new configurations of space and time and eliciting new technological advances in order to navigate those new configurations. The first bicycles reduced the five to six hours taken to walk twenty miles by more than half. Horses could travel that fast, and without the human exertion demanded by the bicycle, but horses had to be maintained, rested, fed, and watered. Bicycles approximated perpetual motion machines. As long as legs supply power, the wheels move. Repetitious, circular motion results in forward movement—progress. The bicycle is a mini-universe, spinning forward against material resistance, taking its rider to a known, and sometimes unknown, destination. And unlike the cadence of human walking or a horse's gait, the bicycle requires the creation of a new surface. Rough places must be smoothed.

In the United States, the first bicycle surfaces were wooden plank rinks where cyclists would only ride in circles, demonstrating their skill to a watching audience. For a brief time, such rinks were profitable businesses, but those rinks could not contain the bicycle. Young men began riding them on sidewalks and roads, frightening pedestrians and horses, prompting many towns and cities to ban bicycles. In the beginning there was no place for the bicycle, no adequate surface. But as bicycles became more popular, they paved the way for new roads, and for the automobile. Of course, the automobile quickly replaced the bicycle as the preferable mode of transportation, of forward progress. As quickly as the bicycle created a new world, that world was taken over by a more powerful and consuming "automotor horse." The automobile also created a world, consuming that of the bicycle and accelerating it, bringing forth unprecedented forward "progress" that involved a greater production and use of energy. It too elicited technological advances: the combustion engine, interstate highways, oil drills, and the assembly line.

The bicycle's dominant world was short-lived, less than half a century. Replaced by the automobile, it never had its opportunity to democratize transportation as its originators hoped it might. It has been, and remains, a source of exercise, recreation, and amusement, primarily for people with means. There are places where it is much more than this; the bicycle has a very different role in China and the Netherlands than it does in the United States, but it could never compete with the automobile and its secularizing and modernizing force, providing rapid progress. The modern era was in too much of a hurry for the bicycle to last long as a mode of transportation. Both the bicycle and automobile are distinctly modern, but they differ markedly in how they construct space and time. Both held forth a similar promise: freedom through autonomous power. For the first time, once the bicycle was invented in the 1860s, people could propel themselves long distances as fast as, if not faster than, a horse could carry them.

The bicycle especially brought freedom for women. They were no longer defined by their geographical space. They could independently move away from spaces they found suffocating. Many people lamented the new freedom. Some denounced women for bicycling. Others relished it. In 1895, the Methodist laywoman, suffragist, and leader in the Woman's Christian Temperance Movement, Frances Willard, learned how to ride a bicycle. She was fifty-six, and it was such a moving experience that she memorialized it in one of the first books on the cultural significance of cycling, *A Wheel Within A Wheel: How I Learned to Ride the Bicycle*. It was a feminist gesture. Riding a bicycle meant a woman could put distance between her and the sphere of domesticity marked out for her. Once women rode bikes, they could travel away from the home and from the clothing cultural mores had previously demanded. Nothing revolutionized women's clothing more than cycling; nothing gave them means to move away like it did. It was why many men frowned on women cycling.

The freedom to "move away" is intrinsic to cycling. When children learn to crawl, walk, or run they remain within their parents' reach. But when they learn to ride a bike, everything is different. Cycling brings the first taste of exceeding a parent's reach, an exhilarating and frightening experience. Fear fills everyone learning to cycle. Balance does not come naturally; it must be learned, and it can only be learned through failure. Cycling and crashing go hand in hand. Cycling is thrilling, even seductive. The allure of the curved bike entices its new owner, drawing them into its liberating world. The center of this new world is a mysterious triangle where the cross bar stretches between two down tubes. Each slender tube is, in itself, insignificant and meaningless, but united in the triangular symmetry that forges the core of the machine, they produce an explosion of power that beckons to be used. The mysterious triangle draws the human body into its symmetry, fitting hands, feet, and torso with mechanical fleshly extensions: handlebars, seat, pedals.

The triangle and its extensions, however, are impotent until they receive power by their connection with a technological innovation that is centuries old, the wheel. Although its invention dates back to 5200 BCE and wheel-drawn vehicles from 4000 BCE, for nearly seven millennia a common means of transport bound human creatures together. In order to progress, to move forward through space, people walked or rode an animal, primarily the horse. Wheels were of limited use without smooth roads. People have always traveled and followed paths others trod before them and with the passage of time those paths became surfaces wheels could more easily traverse, but they lacked efficiency. Paving a path first occurred in Egypt nearly 5,000 years ago. Beginning in the fourth millennium BCE, Romans constructed an elaborate system of paved roads and used carriages to traverse them. No one, however, imagined connecting two wheels together and sitting a person atop them until the nineteenth century. The bicycle represents a convergence between the ancient and modern. Old technologies were put to new uses.

The desire for a "human-powered carriage" arose in the eighteenth century, but it would not be until the nineteenth that inventors experimented with extending the human body's abilities by equipping it with wheels. First came the fated "velocipede," a two-wheeled vehicle propelled by slapping the ground with the rider's feet. It was not well received by the public. An infantile first effort, the velocipede remains as a child's strider

bike. The velocipede gave way to the bicycle when the crank drive and pedals were added to it. Then came pneumatic tires. Experimentation on the
bicycle generated technological revolutions, giving rise to ball bearings,
spoked wheels, and more. It also created new forms of practical knowledge
as persons had to learn to mount and then balance the penny-farthing bicycle with its large front and small rear wheel. The invention of the bicycle
required other forms of technological innovations, roads, mass production,
and bicycle repair garages. Our world is marked by the birth of cycling in
ways we seldom still recognize.

ITINERARIES, MAPS, AND BUFFERED SELVES

Bicycling not only created the world we live in; it makes that world anew.
In the early 1980s, I made three separate journeys from Indiana to California. The first was by bicycle with my college roommate, Bob Engel; that
journey and its significance will be more fully described later in this work.
The second was by car, and the third by plane. Although I covered the same
distance and a similar space, each of those trips structured a different reality.
The philosopher Michel de Certeau distinguishes an itinerary from a map.
A map flattens a journey into spatial points that can be traversed with little
attention to the place that one is traversing. Directions for a map-like journey would be, "Take a left in two miles, then proceed directly for five. When
you come to the T-road, go right." A GPS only gives you a map. If it becomes too absorbing, cyclists miss enjoying the place where they are riding,
a near impossibility given that cycling puts you in a place in a way that other
means of transportation—the automobile, train, or airplane—cannot. A
cyclist knows when there is elevation or inclement weather in a way seldom
available to a driver or passenger in those other means of transportation.
They only traverse the world as the map presents it. An itinerary differs.
Its directions would be more like this, "Ride over the big hill, but watch
out for that pit bull at the yellow house near the top. He'll chase you. When
you come into a clearing, you will find a brook that you can bathe in. You
look like flatlanders. Don't forget how cold it gets on the top of a mountain
when the sun goes down. You will need to keep a fire going if you plan to
sleep outside." (The latter is counsel Bob and I discovered the hard way.) An
itinerary is more helpful in riding a bicycle across the US than a map.

Bob and I graduated from Taylor University in 1982. Life after graduation was uncertain for both of us. He did not have a job and I had been
placed on the waiting list to medical school. He was going to work with a
parachurch organization for the summer in Lake Tahoe, California and had

to be there in early June. He suggested I join him and that we ride our bicycles to California. Without giving it much thought, I said it was a splendid idea and within a few weeks we were headed west on our bicycles. We sold my car for $600 to get enough money for the trip. We had no credit cards, no cell phones, and of course no GPS. No one used helmets back then and although "clipless" bike pedals had been invented, they were primarily used by professionals. We still used toe clips with a strap that you tightened on your shoe. Clipless bike pedals make possible a quick removal of the foot from the pedal; clips with straps require cyclists to bend down and loosen the strap by hand before removing their foot from the pedal. It required both coordination and quickness to avoid falling over, an inevitable and embarrassing occurrence.

We did not plan a specific route; nor did we pack a tent. Our plan was to ask if we could sleep in churches along the way, or we would sleep outdoors with the rain tarp that we packed. We put panniers on our bicycles, loaded them down with what we hoped would be sufficient for the little more than three weeks that we planned to cover the 2,100 miles, and headed west. Because I spent my last semester of college in Haiti I had not ridden a bicycle for four months. Chamois cream would not be developed for another six years. We didn't even have cycling shorts with a good chamois in them. Suffice it to say, it took the first three days of 100-mile riding before we were able to walk normally after dismounting from the bike. It was an adventure.

Bob and I arrived in Lake Tahoe, California after a little more than three demanding weeks of cycling. We were on a strict schedule and took only a few days off. I worked the next three months in a hotel painting and cleaning for the summer. At the end of the summer, I drove back to Indiana with two other persons crammed into a car taking turns driving straight through. It was quick but miserable, just the same stretch of road lying before us for countless hours. We consulted a map but were in no need of an itinerary. Darkness, elevation, wind direction, inclement weather, dogs made little difference. Our bodies were not responsible for the energy that drove us forward. Exits with stations to refill gas and coffee and buy some food were all that were required.

The automobile trip back was no adventure; it was only something to be endured, a mere means of getting from point A to point B. That fall my older sister was married in California and I found myself once again traversing the space between Indiana and California, boarding a plane in Indiana and looking down upon the earth through a view from a window that made it appear unreal, out of reach, the distance marked only by a regulated passing of time, each moment identical to the one before. Traveling by plane makes one an observer of the world rather than a participant in it. The plane, train, and automobile "buffer" the self, protecting it from the elements and from life itself. It is this buffered self that the philosopher Charles Taylor has argued defines the modern, secular self, forming subjects who seek to draw a secure, immanent space around them to protect them from a transcendent fullness of reality that they would otherwise experience. Ride a bicycle through a storm out of necessity or up a mountain to arrive at a destination and that fullness, both in its ferocity and sublimity, cannot but puncture the illusion of the buffered self. Ride a bicycle and the world not only looks but is different.

BALANCING LIFE ON AND OFF THE BIKE

Cycling created a world that I inhabited as fully as I could. I normally rode my bicycle ten to fifteen hours per week. I began my workday early, between 4:30 and 5:30 AM most mornings, so I had sufficient time for all of the day's activities—researching, writing, teaching, meeting with students—and still had time to ride. Then there is the joy of family that takes time and attention. My wife and I raised three children. I rode during those days but made every effort to give family precedence. When our last child left home after twenty-five years of parenting, Ricka and I rediscovered how much we enjoyed each other's company. Marriages and births expanded our family. Each of our son-in-laws is named Adam, and our family has a friendly dispute as to whom is the first and the second Adam. That is theology humor based on St. Paul's teaching and Irenaeus's doctrine of recapitulation. The first Adam is responsible for the fall of humanity and the second for its redemption. For Irenaeus, the second Adam recapitulates creation in his life, healing its wounds. "Recapitulates" means that the second Adam takes up the work of the first, even in its failures, and begins it anew.

Our Adams add much to our life, bringing their friends and family into our circle. Our family continued to expand as we added granddaughters Harper, Sophie, and Emma. When my daughter Lindsey was in the hospital giving birth to Emma, our family friend who is like a member of our family and a strong cyclist, Lily, rode bicycles with me to the hospital as we waited for Emma's arrival. Lily lived with us for several years and we often rode together. Four foot ten inches short, she has more power packed into her than many cyclists I know. All told, then, family relationships take time. Not only my wife, but also my family, indulged my cycling habits, but I tried not to let them interfere with what mattered most—them.

I must confess that I was not always successful in keeping cycling from consuming a proper life balance. When Becky got engaged to her Adam, my mother planned a shower for the last weekend in July. Ricka informed me that we would be going. I looked at her and said, "But that is the weekend of the Windy 500," an annual ride with ten to twenty cycling buddies who ride more than 500 miles in four days. Started by my friend Jason Kayzar to celebrate his birthday, it was one of my favorite cycling events each year, along with the 160-mile Bone Ride from Milwaukee to Madison and back (it will be discussed more fully in chapter 4), the 200-plus mile Ride Across Wisconsin, the periodic double century from Milwaukee to Chicago and back, and various long-distance rallies. I scheduled family and professional events so that I would be available for these rides. Our anniversary was also the last weekend in July, and we had celebrated for five consecutive years on a different date so I could ride the Windy. Ricka indulged that, but this latest objection was too much. The moment I heard those words come out of my mouth I knew I had made a serious error in judgment. Ricka looked at me quizzically, shook her head, and before she could say the words that she had every right to say, I supplemented my comment by saying, "But of course I won't do it this year. Becky's shower is more important."

In 1981, two years before I married Ricka, I completed a half-Ironman and always wanted to complete a full. Marriage, graduate school, and then children kept putting it off. When I turned forty in 2000 I decided it was now or never and began biking, running, swimming, and lifting weights. I had more than doubled my usual workout time from two to four or five hours daily. My children were fourteen, eleven, and nine. After one month of such time-consuming training, I realized that this was not how I wanted to live; family, teaching, church, and academic duties were more important. I abandoned the goal of completing the full Ironman without any regret. I have not been in a pool to swim long distances since.

Every hardcore cyclist knows about the 95 Velominati Rules. These rules arise from statements made by legendary cyclists and express stylistic features of the form and content of cycling. For instance, eyewear is always to be worn, and worn outside the helmet straps. Tan lines should be cut, reflecting that the rider has spent considerable time riding outdoors. A cyclist's tan lines are unique, including not only the cut lines at mid-thigh and mid-upper arm from a kit, but also the outlines of cycling gloves and even the helmet straps on the cyclist's cheeks. Kits should be called kits, and they must always match, but not with the socks. Bicycles are never to be lifted over one's head nor turned upside down and rested on the seat. Rule #12 states that the number of bikes one should own is "n + 1" (if you own four, you should own five and if you own five you should own six, etc.). Rule #11 is "Family does not come first. The bike does." When someone says they cannot ride because of family obligations, a proper response is to invoke rule #11. Yet every nonprofessional cyclist, which are most cyclists that you will ever ride with, knows that this rule, like all the others, is intended to be humorous. Each of the 95 rules should be offset by rule #43, "don't be a jackass." The rules are intended to be broken, unless you already violated rule #43, and plenty of type A cyclists do. Juggling family, church, life as a scholar, and finding time to ride was demanding. Only a fool, or possibly a professional at the top of the sport, would put cycling before these other more important obligations.

I have also had the great privilege of advising more than thirty doctoral students in my scholarly vocation; there is little that brings as much joy as watching them progress toward the completion of their degree and then taking their place as scholars and teachers. Advising doctoral students is a time-consuming duty of delight. Students make advisors better scholars than they could ever be by themselves, because advisors need to read not only their work but also what their advisees are reading. It takes work to stay ahead of eager and talented graduate students. I also teach seminarians and undergraduates and find it richly rewarding. I am always surprised that I earn a good living doing what I so thoroughly enjoy.

Riding, researching, writing, teaching, and family, as well as church commitments, take time. Setting priorities and keeping perspective on what matters most says more about one's loves than one's subjective utterances. Whether or not I too often placed cycling above other more important commitments is not a judgment that is finally mine to make. My wife and children are best positioned to give an answer. One thing is certain: after October 11, 2020 and for at least the foreseeable future, I gained time. I lost the busyness that had become a habit of forcing too many things in a single day.

THE SURPRISING GRACE OF A SCHOLARLY VOCATION

As someone who grew up in rural Indiana, becoming a university professor was not something I had countenanced. That I rode a bicycle for forty years is less unusual than that I became a scholar. Oddly enough, where I come from, the former, even with the shaven legs (Velominati rule #33), is less objectionable than a life devoted to reading and writing. My parents were unusual in that they supported the life of the mind, but our family had no acquaintance with any professors. I met my first one when I went off to college, but even then it did not occur to me that such a possibility was open to me. Stanley Hauerwas, Gilbert T. Rowe Emeritus Professor of Theological Ethics at Duke Divinity School, first suggested to me that I should pursue a doctorate, in my second year of seminary. Until that moment, it never occurred to me that it was something I could do. I did not know how to go about it. Stanley walked me through the process.

I went to college primarily interested in running. If my ability to be a long-distance runner had not been taken away from me, I would have never discovered that I was fit for scholarly life. From this painful and difficult experience, new possibilities emerged. I enjoy, without apology, my vocation as a professor and life as a scholar. I love what I do, but I am still surprised that it came to be. As a young boy, nothing but basketball appealed to me. My father began his career as a basketball coach and a biology teacher in Indiana, where basketball was an art form. Without the ability to shoot, dribble, make a no-look pass, and sink free throws, young people lacked social status. We were regaled with stories of great basketball victories like that of rural Milan high school that won the 1954 high school state championship, defeating many larger urban schools. We seldom thought about the racial implications of such stories. The movie *Hoosiers* told that story with Blacks sitting in the stands in white rural Indiana towns. Nope, that most likely did not happen in "sundown" towns. Whites could play in Black areas, but Blacks were seldom welcome in white ones and they had to be out of town before the sun set. Basketball, like many sports, nonetheless generated forms of life that brought Blacks and whites together. The high school state basketball championship rivaled Easter as the central liturgical event making life meaningful. The glory and honor acquired on the basketball court was equivalent to what could be earned by fighting on the field of battle or serving in missionary lands. Nearly every young Indiana boy would practice his final midcourt shot counting down 3–2–1 as time expired and he launched the ball from midcourt until it swished through the net, winning the game and propelling his name into basketball lore.

During elementary school, I would stay on the school bus until it concluded its trip by pulling into the high school. My dad would be holding basketball practice and he would let me think that I was working out with the team. I wanted nothing more than to play basketball. My parents placed two pictures on the wall in my bedroom, the periodic chart of the elements and a picture of Oscar Robertson, the Big O, who grew up in Indiana and became a sensational NBA player. At six feet five inches, the Big O was two inches shorter than the average professional basketball player, but still one foot taller than me. To say the least, my prospects as a basketball player were limited, and my parents knew it. Dad enjoyed sport but learned not to take it too seriously. My mother never thought much of it. They encouraged me to study rather than pursue the illusory glory of athletics. Education helped my dad overcome the poverty of his childhood; his life's vocation was to make education as widely available as possible, beginning with his children and wife. He encouraged Mom to get her college degree as soon as he finished his; she postponed it while raising four children, waiting to enter college the year after I did. We studied chemistry together.

Despite my parents' warnings about my limited future prospects, I threw myself into basketball and sought to overcome my limitations by developing the ability to run farther and faster than other players on the court. I ran extra laps after practice in hopes that my ability to hustle would garner a position on the starting five. In the off season, I joined the cross-country team solely for the purpose of staying in shape for basketball. At first, I loathed running. No one enjoys running when they first take it up; it is painful. The body is not naturally made for it. The runner whose efforts gave rise to the marathon, Pheidippides (530–490 BCE), ran the twenty-five miles from Marathon to Athens to let the Greeks know of their victory over the Persians—and then died. Otherwise healthy people die unexpectedly in marathons.

Long-distance running is an ascetic discipline and an acquired habit. Training requires foregoing comforts and pleasures in an effort to develop a second nature capable of overcoming the suffering long-distance exercise brings. Running is an Augustinian endeavor. St. Augustine argued that human creatures were responsible for the evil that befell them but that the good they could do was attributable to God's grace. Running is kind of like that. A runner suffers through self-inflicted pain to reach a level where running no longer causes as much suffering, as if the runner had attained a level of grace that makes running effortless. Once that state is attained, it must be maintained or it quickly dissipates, requiring the repetition of the self-inflicted pain yet again to attain that state. It takes months to get fit and only a few weeks to lose it. No matter how much someone trains, they never come to the place where they arrive. Daily exercise cannot be neglected without losing the connatural ability to run long distances. Perhaps it is the endorphins, or the self-knowledge involved in acquiring that second nature, but for some reason those who develop the ability for distance exercise eventually find it addicting. Over time I realized that I was better at running than playing basketball. Thus, I became an avid runner. What began as training for basketball became an end in itself.

I began running at thirteen years of age. Losing the ability to run at the age of eighteen was my first significant loss. Unlike my mother, very little had been taken from me during childhood or my teenage years. Her mother died when she was five and her stepmother when she was eleven. Mom lived with siblings and was moved from home to home. Compared to her, my life was intact, a stable home life with loving parents. There had been the motorcycle accident at fifteen, which marked me and still needs to be told, but I had experienced no broken bones, no significant illnesses, no surgeries, no death of a close family member or friend until I was eighteen. We were not wealthy, but we never experienced grinding poverty. A basketball coach in Indiana has tenuous job security. My father frequently changed jobs, seldom by choice, but we were never refugees. The sad plight that inflicts so many was never ours. We had a privileged, stable home life.

Although we regularly moved, my parents owned a summer cabin on Lake Shafer in Buffalo, Indiana where my father and I were born. I worked in the summers at a business started by my uncle, Buffalo Park Discount House. I did not enjoy it primarily because it cut into my time for training. I once asked my parents if I could forego my usual summer job and spend the time training. They said no. I later asked them if they required me to work so that I would learn the value of labor. Dad replied, "No, we needed the money for your college education." The summer before college, I ran the best 15k race of my life. High expectations accompanied me to the pre-season cross-country "miracle camp" consisting of four daily workouts and where I first met Bob. For a runner, miracle camp was nirvana, nothing to do but devote oneself to training. I started off the season well. Things quickly went south.

Halfway through my first college cross-country season, running became painful. A dull, aching but consistent pain shot from my lower back into my right hip and leg. Perhaps I had been overtraining? Resting a few days made no difference. I rested a few more, and then more, but nothing changed. Doctors could not explain what was going on. Perhaps it was psychological? Maybe if I tried harder I could overcome the weakness overtaking me. Increased training only brought on more pain and diminished capacity. I was losing the ability to run without an adequate explanation. This went on for months. The dull, physical pain affected my mental health. I became unmotivated to do anything. I finished up that first year of college with a less than stellar grade point average. My parents took me to see an orthopedic specialist, who then sent me to a neurosurgeon. They put me through a number of tests and discovered an extra iliac crest on the right side of my pelvis that was fused with the lower vertebrae. This congenital bony growth had deteriorated my spine, pinching the nerves into my leg. They suggested surgery to fuse the bones more fully to stabilize them and to widen the foramina to free the nerves.

Surgery was planned for December 1979. It took seven hours, followed by three weeks of bed rest and months in a plaster then plastic cast from my armpits to below my pelvis. It was grueling. The second semester of my sophomore year was spent wearing that cast. I could not run or exercise at all. I had a limited social life. The one thing I could do was study. Reading every class assignment and studying for tests, I made a remarkable discovery. A direct correlation exists between the effort put into learning and the results achieved. My grades went from mediocre to straight A's. More important than the grades, I discovered the joy of learning. Being well prepared for class made the professors more interesting. The loss of running led to the discovery of scholarship. Like the beginning of many good things, it too came about by contingent acts, an unexpected gift.

THE BIRTH OF MY CYCLING; THE CYCLES OF MY BIRTH

The semester spent in a body cast was not easy. Basic functions like putting on shoes were burdensome. Bob Engels and I had become roommates. My classes began before his, especially my early morning chemistry lab. Without asking, he set his alarm, rose early, and made sure my shoes were on and I was ready for the day. Our friendship grew closer as he bore with me that difficult semester, easing its burden. Once the cast was removed, he supported me through my recovery. Running remained a goal and I longed to return to the cross-country team. But when the cast came off, running was still impossible; my body could not yet take the jarring. Waiting for the day when I would run again, I mounted an old single-speed bicycle, the only one I owned, and began riding to recover aerobic fitness in preparation for the day I would once again take up running. As I waited for that day, cycling became routine. I discovered that cycling kept my muscles toned, alleviating back pain, which motivated me then and for the next forty years to ride. Cycling and core exercise prevented the otherwise frequent back injuries. To maintain what had now become a regular cycling routine, a more advanced bike was necessary. I purchased a Schwinn Le Tour and began to ride regularly, still hoping that I would be able to take up running again.

Easing back into running my junior year, I continued the cycling, alternating days between them. Knowing that I was running and cycling, a friend told me about a triathlon scheduled in the fall of 1981 in a town near our university. It was the half-Ironman that I mentioned previously: a one-and-one-quarter-mile swim followed by fifty-six miles of cycling and finishing with a thirteen-mile run. What better way to prove my triumphant return as a long-distance athlete than to complete a half-Ironman? One year after having my cast removed, I trained in earnest. An older cousin now operated Buffalo Park Discount House and he gave me a summer job working as the cashier. I lived at my parents' cabin.

My parents had purchased their cabin on Lake Shafter in 1974. It is the most stable and consistent home that I have had in my life. I lived there alone in the summer of 1981, working and doing little more than running, cycling, and swimming to prepare for the triathlon. I would bicycle to work, come home and run, and swim in the river. Lake Shafer is not really a lake; it is the Tippecanoe River that was dammed in the 1920s. I spent nearly every summer in high school and college living there and running along the river each day, going from my parents' cabin south to Lowes Bridge, turning back north until Buffalo Bridge, and then back south to the cabin, a thirteen-mile run. It remains one of my favorite places to cycle. I know every farm road within a fifty-mile radius. Buffalo is where I began. For better or worse, it is a place to which I return year after year. No matter how far away I live, it calls me home. It taught me virtues and instilled in me lingering vices. We inherit both from our histories, and everyone's inheritance is as distinct as their personal histories.

Like my father, I was born in Buffalo, Indiana in White County, a place so small that people in Indiana cannot locate it on a map. Hoosiers (Indiana residents) only fifty miles away have seldom heard of it. But Buffalo was an enchanted place for me. Boating, fishing, rafting, floating the river, collecting turtles and frogs, and being tended to by parents, aunts, uncles, and grandparents occupied my childhood. My grandfather and grandmother on my mother's side were the first of their family to live in Buffalo. They left Indianapolis to begin a fishing resort in 1943 on the banks of the Tippecanoe River in an area known as Buffalo Park. They had seven children, three boys and four girls, and built seven cottages naming each cottage after one of their children. I was born when my parents were living in one of those cottages shortly after they returned from France, where my father had been stationed in the Army for two years. My mother was the seventh child, eight years behind her closest sibling and twenty-two behind her eldest. Her mother died at the age of forty-three when my mother was five. Her father provided for her, but he had no idea what to do with a five-year-old, so he sent her to live with different siblings throughout her childhood. My uncles were hard drinkers, heavy smokers, and excellent fishermen. My mother recalls one of my uncles with whom she stayed who came home drunk, got his gun, and in an angry stupor, fired it into the ceiling when she and her niece were sleeping upstairs. No one knew why; he most likely resented being asked to take her in.

My grandmother had been a faithful member of the Evangelical United Brethren Church (EUB) in Indianapolis before moving to Buffalo; I've been told that she would have been proud that her grandson and great granddaughter became United Methodist ministers. My oldest daughter and I are United Methodist ministers. I'd like to think that we carry on a tradition my grandmother initiated, although I only know of her through my aunts' stories. My mother did not know her mother. She has no story to tell. It was a loss she bore all her life, a lasting fracture that generated a fear of abandonment, a sense that loss was right around the corner.

The "United" in United Methodist comes from a merger between the EUB and the Methodists. As a United Methodist elder, I co-officiated the wedding ceremony for one of my aunts who married her childhood sweetheart in her eighties, after her first husband died. The wedding was in the former EUB church that my grandmother attended in Indianapolis. This aunt was a character whom I dearly loved, as I did another aunt, who was a beautician and always gave me free haircuts, but more importantly, free counsel. My aunts were much easier to be around than my uncles. I co-officiated both aunts' funerals and celebrate their lives whenever I remember them. They were kind, gentle, and inviting. A third aunt, however, scared me. She seemed cold and distant, always on her guard as if someone were about to take advantage of her. Don't get me wrong, she was kind to me, but there was something aloof that kept her from the warm embraces my other aunts regularly doled out. As a child, I did not understand it; I just knew to keep some distance. When I became an adult, I was given the reason. She had been married to an abusive man who would lock her in a room when he went to work out of a perverse sense of possessiveness, and not unlock it until he returned. She lived at a time when a man could do such things without consequences. She left him once, only to return. I find that unfathomable, but it happened. Thankfully, she divorced him a second time. When I was first confronted with feminist critiques of patriarchy in seminary, they made sense because I knew that stories like this were true.

I did not know my uncles on my mom's side well. Two of them died of heart disease in their early fifties before I was a teenager. No one knows exactly what they died of. Perhaps I carry similar genetic abnormalities. Because they were heavy drinkers, smokers, and seldom exercised, I may have assumed that my fate would not be the same as theirs. In truth, however, I never gave much thought to it except on those occasions when a physician asked if there was heart disease in the family. "Only the uncles on my mother's side," I would say. That never seemed to bother the physician. I never smoked and regularly exercised; perhaps unconsciously and erroneously, I imagined that the uncles deserved their fate, as if the world was a reasonable place in which vice leads to an untimely end and virtue to a long, happy life? I know better. I know that is a false, presumptuous attitude, but the assumption that right living could avoid my uncles' fate was an illusion that, however unconsciously held, was punctured October 11, 2020 when I realized that what I thought was helping me avoid their fate might have contributed to my almost sharing it. I may have avoided it only because of advances in cardiac care.

A third uncle had alcohol and drug addictions coupled with mental illness. He was homeless because of his many problems, having alienated his wife, children, and family. My father, who is kind to everyone, would not let him come around our place. The only time I saw my uncle show up at my parents' cabin, my dad asked him to leave. I was surprised to see this side of him, but he knew that my uncle could not be trusted. The uncle was fortunate to be homeless in Buffalo, Indiana, where people looked after him. He would live in fishing shacks by the water. My mother once took me with her to find him on Thanksgiving; she heard that he was in a particular place down by the river and she checked in to see how he was doing. He said he was fine. He had some kind of animal, a possum or raccoon, cooking in a crock pot. He outlived my other uncles by twenty years.

My grandfather's fishing resort did not last long. Buffalo is two to three hours from Chicago and Chicagoans purchased many of the former fishing homes on the river turning them into summer cottages. Compared to Chicago, property is cheap in White County. The new residents were less interested in fishing than boating and water skiing. My grandfather sold Buffalo Park to his oldest son. My uncle sold off the cottages and began Buffalo Park Discount House, a plumbing and lumber store that catered to people who owned the summer cottages. When my uncle died, his sons inherited it. Several of my cousins worked there at some point or another. One summer while I was working there, we heard fire engines and wondered what was going on. Later I was informed that my homeless uncle had purchased a car but had no license for it or himself. He was pulled over by the sheriff, who then informed him that without licenses he could not drive the car. Angry, he returned to the parked car and set it on fire. He then realized that his fishing tackle box was in the trunk and called the fire squad to put it out; they declined.

My grandfather and his oldest son had money, at least according to the standards of Buffalo, Indiana. They had properties in Florida and drove nice cars, but the family wealth was unequally distributed and that caused resentful feelings among the siblings. My father's family had a very different experience. They were poor farmers and factory workers. He was the oldest of five, two brothers and two sisters. Like my mother, he knew loss as a child. His father never returned from World War II. He didn't die; he just did not come back to Indiana. Nor did he see military action. He never left Camp Croft, South Carolina but took up with another woman and started a family with her unbeknownst to my grandmother. When she found out, she was devastated. She and her five children moved in with her mother and father, Maude and Clarence Conwell, and helped them on the farm. The Conwells were family; "Long" was nothing but a name my father and I bear. The Conwell farm was on the backwater of the Tippecanoe River, one of my favorite places in the world, filled with frogs, turtles, large carp, and muck that would suck you into its grip past your knees. The farm is a stone's throw from my parents' cabin but was sold and turned into a summer home years ago. Now, no one would know it was once an active farm.

My grandmother Thelma was a small farmer, but there was not much "small" to her except the family farm. She was a short, large woman. When she hugged you as a child you would disappear for a significant time only to reemerge renewed by her love. She had a difficult but nonetheless joyful life. She never drove a car. Her brother tried to teach her once and she crashed, never to attempt it again. The family had pigs and chickens. Her chickens were free range only because they had bad chicken wire. The chickens ran all over the farm. Grandmother Thelma also had wild cats that lived in solidarity with the chickens in the chicken coop. They were as mean as any chickens, who are some of the meanest animals God ever created. Chickens are fascists, which might be why they have a "pecking order." As a boy, I feared that chicken coop as if it were the gate of hell. "Abandon all hope, ye who enter here." I admired grandmother because she had no fear of the wild cats or chickens. She would enter into the coop without fear and trembling. I went with her when she would start the preparations for Sunday dinner by grabbing one of those chickens, wringing its neck, placing her foot on it, and popping off its head. It would flop around making a scene that when you witness it as a young child stays with you. The hogs were less scary. They would come running as happy as could be when you would slop them, calling out "suey, suey."

Grandma Thelma and her free-range chickens.

The family farm was not sustaining, making it necessary for grandmother to go to work at a local factory, laboring there for three decades and retiring without any pension or retirement fund. The family who owned it, of course, considered themselves job creators with little mutual affirmation that the workers were the ones who made their business possible. Because she did not drive nor own a car, a coworker took her to work. She required Thelma to walk to the main road, one and one-half miles away. I know the distance because I ran that route for years. When Thelma's parents died, the farm was sold. My dad purchased a modular home and put it on property he owned close to our cabin and the Conwell farm. Grandmother lived there for quite some time with her friend Mel, with whom she lived for twenty years. They were never married; I have no idea to this day what the status of their relationship was. Mel was on oxygen and the tube for it was always lying haphazardly on the floor. My siblings and I would accidentally step on it and Mel would cry out, "Get off the tube, kids," which was alarming. We did not know if we were causing him to lose his breath, restricting his movement, or if he was messing with us. He was kind and liked to talk politics and baseball. As a child, I thought nothing of their relationship. It seemed normal. I'm glad grandmother had a companion. Perhaps they were mere friends (I doubt it)? Perhaps she did not believe in marriage after divorce? Perhaps they could not afford to marry given that it would lessen their social security checks? Her life reminds me that things get broken and are not easily put back together. Sometimes, all we can do is muddle through the best we can.

My absent grandfather Long was not known for paying child support. When he would return to Indiana, Thelma would have him arrested, which did not encourage him to pay child support or return to Indiana. Grandmother would not let his name be mentioned in her presence. When it was, she broke down. In fact, I did not know his name until I was an adult. I honored her sentence of excommunication and never would have violated it by stating his name in her presence or inquiring about him. She removed him from our life. I recall my dad talking about him on one of our many fishing excursions: "Son, you know it takes more than getting a woman pregnant to be a father." Rightly or wrongly, grandfather Long became a negative moral example of what it meant to be a parent, husband, family member. I still know nothing about him. He showed up unexpected once at our home in Fishers, Indiana and I will never forget how my father introduced him: "Son, this is your grandfather." He did not refer to him as his father. He did not attend my grandfather's funeral.

Because my father's family was poor, my dad would be farmed out to another family in the summers during his high school years to live with them and help work their farm, driving a tractor to help with the crops. I always found it odd that he remembers this time fondly. He has collected tractors all his life even though he has little use for them. He keeps them at the cabin and brings them out primarily to give his grand- and great-grandchildren rides. Those tractors remind him of his roots. The family to whom he was farmed out sat together for evening family meals. He would be required to sit at a table with linen, be properly attired, and eat with the appropriate utensils. It made a striking impression on him and perhaps was a reason we always had family dinners at the dining room table. At the end of the summer, they would purchase clothes for him for the upcoming school year and then he would return to the small farm with his mother, grandmother, and grandfather.

Several of my dad's uncles were war heroes. One had fought in the Battle of the Bulge and was berated by General Paton for getting his bulldozer stuck in Belgium. Another had been shot down over Germany and spent time in a prisoner-of-war camp. He was a mechanic in the Army Air Corps; no air force existed at the time. On that fateful day the tail gunner fell ill, and my great uncle was ordered to take his place. His plane was shot down, but he parachuted safely to the ground and was immediately captured. We have had many family gatherings over the years and I never heard my great uncle discuss any of this. He tended to be silent, seldom initiating conversation. Toward the end of his life, he attended a family reunion and was uncharacteristically chatting away while sitting at the children's table. My children, who were then teenagers, were sitting near him and he told them a story that my father did not know. It was unclear if he had told anyone. The Russians liberated his prisoner-of-war camp and took the German guards captive. The commanding Russian officer looked at my great uncle, who suffered terribly as a prisoner of war, and asked how the German officer in charge treated the prisoners. He told him, and the Russian officer handed his gun to my great uncle and said, "Be judge, jury, and executioner." Sitting at that table and telling this story, he held the attention of everyone within hearing range. "I shot him in the head." The room fell silent. The story was over; we went back to our meal. He died a few years later. Why he told that story at that time to that audience remains a mystery.

My parents, Sue and Wayne, were thirteen and sixteen when they started dating. Four years later, in 1956, they were married. Wayne was stationed at Fort Gordon, Georgia while he awaited his deployment to France. He entered the military to receive the GI Bill so that he could go to college when he got out. By the time he did, the government had done away with the GI Bill. He went to school anyway and Sue helped him pay for it. They decided to get married before he deployed. He was twenty; she was seventeen. He acquired a three-day pass to come home, marry her, and then headed off to France the next month where he was stationed for two and one-half years. Sue followed two months later on the USS Homeric. Wayne spent his deployment playing basketball and fixing radios. When his service was ended, they returned to Buffalo with my older sister Diane, who had been born in France; they had me shortly thereafter.

WHITE COUNTY LEGACIES

Although I was born in "White County," it never occurred to me how significant it was that a picture of an African American hero adorned my walls and aspirations during my childhood. It was the late sixties and the civil rights movement was in full force, but you would not have known that in rural Indiana. I remember a trip down South to visit relatives and seeing segregated bathrooms and drinking fountains, but the transformation occurring in the country affected us little. Like many Indiana children in White County, I grew up hearing racist remarks from family members. Although the county was named after a prominent family named White, its name had taken on a racist narrative. The American Legion held a boxing match in Monticello, the closest town to Buffalo, on October 30, 1947 and managed to arrange for Joe Louis to fight an unknown heavyweight. Because Monticello was at least unofficially a sundown town, Louis was not allowed to spend the night but required to return to Indianapolis after the match. My father remembers discussing it with his grandfather Clarence Conwell, who said that was unjust. I was told that story as a child on several occasions. I never knew my great-grandfather Clarence and wonder why he knew it was wrong, but he would have been the exception. Other family members would certainly have supported it.

"White" County took on a significance beyond its original meaning among some of those family members. Jesse Jackson began his campaign for presidency the same year that I headed for seminary. At a family gathering I mentioned that I planned to vote for him, to the surprise of one of my uncles. He was incensed and responded, "I'd kill that n***er if I could get away with it." To think that such sentiment was a minority opinion in White County is to live an illusion. My parents never indulged such vitriol. My father only spanked me twice in my life, once because I forgot to feed the dog for an entire day after he told me to do so. He came home from work and asked if I had done what he asked. I told him the truth. "No, I had not," and he said, "Son, that is a living thing. You cannot treat a living thing like that. Get my paddle." Walking to get the paddle was worse than the paddling itself. The second time was when he heard me say the n-word, a word I repeated after having heard it at elementary school. I had no idea at the time what that word meant, nor did I understand my father's reaction, but I knew I had done something horrible and never repeated it again. I would like to say that the church challenged the racism prevalent from my father's childhood, but that would be a lie. In the 1930s in central Indiana a significant number of clergy were either members or supporters of the Ku Klux Klan.[1] My dad's time in the military challenged the racism he grew up with. His first bunkmate in basic training was his first African American acquaintance. They became friends and my dad decided then and there that if they could both die for their country they should be entitled to the same rights. Would that the church thought the same about baptism.

I was raised to consider the racist language common in White County, oddly enough even among my family, the domain of southerners and the ignorant. Educated people did not indulge such coarse language. I naively thought most educated northerners had overcome racism. We lived in Goshen, Indiana among the Amish, Mennonites, and Brethren for a few years in the late sixties and early seventies. It was the height of the Vietnam War and a Goshen College student, a conscientious objector, stayed with us for a brief time. I remember family discussions about war. My parents were kind to him, but at that time they disagreed with his stance. Racism and white supremacy were seldom discussed in our school or neighborhood. Our elementary school took a field trip to a home that was on the Underground Railroad and had the room where runaways slaves were hidden. It never occurred to me that I, my friends, and even family, would not have been on the right side of history. It was only after college that I discovered how deeply the state of Indiana was involved in the Ku Klux Klan and the vicious ideology of white supremacy, something that I consider more intractable than racism and the condition for its possibility.

White County is part of my history; I cannot shake it nor would I desire to dispense with all that I learned growing up. I inherited virtues from being born there and also vices, and one is the vice of "whiteness." By that, I do not mean to be self-loathing or condemnatory of white people. "White" does not name a race; it is not a biological identification. It is a culture, a construct that, fortunately, can be other. James Baldwin wrote, "Negroes in this country—and Negroes do not, strictly or legally speaking exist in any other—are taught really to despise themselves from the moment their eyes open on the world. This world is white and they are black. White people hold the power, which means that they are superior to blacks (intrinsically, that is: God decreed it so)."[2] White is the political power to create sundown towns and prevent Blacks from inhabiting them. But white is also forgetfulness, the loss of history, the failure to recognize that all our lives come with histories. White is the ability to say, "I never owned slaves" and yet still position yourself with the privilege whiteness entails.

Just as Baldwin recognized that "Negroes" only exist in the US, it is also at least partly correct to say that whiteness primarily exists here. This political and cultural distinction was at the birth of this nation, reinscribed at its rebirth in Jim Crow, and constantly repeated in new and different ways such as mass incarceration and "America First!" It affected cycling, excluding one of America's greatest riders, Major Taylor, from competing in his own country. It permeates everything, perhaps like Catholic and Protestant does Northern Ireland.

While on the faculty of St. Joseph's University, a Jesuit university in Philadelphia, I had the privilege to teach a course entitled "Violence, Peace, and Reconciliation" in Northern Ireland. We read works throughout the semester on forgiveness and then took primarily Catholic students to live in Protestant households to inquire how this deep division was being dismantled before and after "the Troubles" that tore that nation apart. Our hope in teaching the course was that students might learn something about divisions in the US. There is a story told in Northern Ireland about a Protestant militia man who confronted a taxi driver and asked him if he was a Protestant or Catholic. His response was, "I'm neither. I'm Jewish." The man then asked him, "Yes, but are you a Protestant or Catholic Jew?" The parallel does not fit exactly, but it can nonetheless be illuminating. The US is constructed on a binary of white/Black, which is less about color and more about supremacy and domination. Even if you are a poor white, this binary is available to you. It allows whites to travel freely when non-whites were at first legally restricted from certain areas and later had to be cautious in those same areas. I seldom need to think about this history when I mount my bicycle for a ride. My Black friends who ride do not have that luxury.

WHITE SUPREMACY'S STRANGE FRUIT

I went to high school in Wabash, Indiana, thirty-five miles north of where I went to college at Taylor University in Upland; Marion lies between the towns, closer to Upland than Wabash. One of the most notorious lynchings in US history occurred in Marion, on August 7, 1930. It inspired Abel Meeropol's famous poem "Strange Fruit," which Billie Holiday set to music in her haunting 1939 song by that name. When Meeropol saw a photo of the lynching, he wrote:

> Southern trees bear a strange fruit
> Blood on the leaves and blood at the root
> Black body swinging in the Southern breeze
> Strange fruit hanging from the poplar trees

But the photo was not from the South; it was from central Indiana. In fact, per capita, a similar percentage of lynchings of Black people occurred in the North as in the South. The photo Meeropol saw was of two African American men from Marion, Thomas Shipp, nineteen years of age, and Abram Smith, eighteen.

Shipp and Smith went out joyriding that fateful evening, and brought along the younger James Cameron, sixteen years of age. Shipp and Smith had set out to steal a car and found Claude Deeter, who was twenty-four, and Mary Ball, eighteen, parked on River Road. Smith told Cameron to hold the gun while they committed the robbery. Cameron became frightened and ran away, confessing that he momentarily held the gun but had nothing to do with the robbery or subsequent murder. He heard three shots as he headed for home when either Shipp or Smith shot Deeter, who later died of his wounds. The evil of Deeter's murder was revenged by the unjust lynching of Shipp, Smith, and the attempted lynching of Cameron. There was no trial, no investigation, no legal statements of what occurred.

Claude Deeter's parents witnessed to a powerful sense of forgiveness and they not only refused to participate in the unjust lynching but also denounced it. They were devout Christians, involved with a Quaker sect, who objected to capital punishment and made a public statement against the events that transpired after their son was murdered. On August 8, the following statement was issued:

> Deep regret that the negro slayers of their son Claude, were lynched in Marion last night by a mob was expressed today by Mr. and Mrs. William Deeter, members of the Apostolic faith, a sect similar to Quakers. "God should have been the judge," said the elderly Deeter. "They had no right to do it," his wife assented. Both are opposed to capital punishment and did not want to see the negroes put to death for their crime.[3]

Shipp, Smith, and Cameron were also accused of raping Ball, a claim she denied at Cameron's trial, although unlike the Deeters she lodged no objection to the lynching and was quoted saying, "They got what they deserved."[4]

Shipp, Smith, and Cameron were arrested, beaten, and thrown in the Grant County Jail. Central Indiana was known for its large Klan population. One-fourth to one-third of all white men in Indiana were thought to be members in 1925. Cameron had only lived in Marion for two years. Previously, he lived briefly with his family in Wabash. Now he found himself in jail while a lynch mob gathered outside. He observed a large crowd of white folk gathering out his cell window with a heightening sense of trepidation as his fellow prisoners, most imprisoned for hopping a freight train as part of the northern migration, discussed his possibility of being lynched. The lynching was neither spontaneous nor secret; it was what was known as a "spectacle lynching," having been planned and advertised over radio stations in the Midwest in order to draw a large crowd to Marion. The Klan and others decided to take matters into their own hands. Everyone paying attention knew what was about to happen. The local NAACP tried to stop it, asking the governor and Marion's mayor to intervene, but to no avail.

Cameron watched out the cell window as up to 15,000 whites gathered. He recognized a few faces, including some of his school classmates. The mob first attempted to burn down the jail to force the three men out but failed. Then they broke into the jail, dragged out Shipp and Smith, and beat Shipp nearly to death. He may have revived right before they hung him. Smith was most likely beaten to death before he was hung. The crowd then came for Cameron but the people who stormed the jail were uncertain who he was. Other Black prisoners refused to give him up even though the machine gun-toting leader threatened to hang every one of them. An elderly man, bending down on his knees, told the gun-toting leader that Cameron was not in the jail. He was kicked in the face, knocking out many teeth. Another man jailed along with his son, was threatened to be hung with his son. Taking the threat to his son seriously, he finally yielded and pointed to Cameron.

Grabbed, hit, kicked, spat upon, and bitten by children, Cameron was dragged out of the jail to the lynching tree to join Shipp and Smith. Cameron looked for a kind face in the crowd, a gesture seeking some reassurance of humanity. The rope was placed around his neck and he momentarily slipped into unconsciousness. He awoke praying for mercy. A woman's voice cried out, "Take this boy back. He had nothing do with any raping or killing!" Only Cameron heard that voice. In interviews after the fact, Cameron could find no other person who heard it. Nor did anyone have an adequate explanation why the crowd relented and let him limp and stumble back to the jail. For Cameron, it was a "miraculous intervention."[5] He was then sent to adult prison in Anderson, Indiana and served four years (five altogether, one awaiting trial) of a sentence of not less than two nor more than twenty-one years. He was released on a five-year parole at twenty-one years of age. Sheriff Bradley, a Roman Catholic from Elwood, Indiana, the heart of the Klan, supported Cameron in jail, even giving him release time to come to his home for family meals. Bradley made a deep and lasting impression on Cameron, who converted to Catholicism later in life and gave credit to Bradley, whose kindness was so significant for him. Cameron moved to Milwaukee and used his life savings to begin America's Black Holocaust Museum. He died in 2006.

I went to high school and university within twenty miles of the courthouse where Shipp and Smith were lynched. I bicycled through the place where this horrifying event occurred countless times but was blithely unaware of its history. Neither the university nor high school that I attended taught me about it; nor did they challenge me with the legacy of white supremacy that permeated the soil, a legacy still present during my Taylor days.

In 1981 I had bicycled around Lake Michigan with a roommate, who was from the Masai tribe in Kenya. He was tall and stately compared to my short and unimposing frame. As an African new to the US, he was often unaware of the racism present in central Indiana. We trained for our trip one summer while working together in a local home for boys. We would go out riding in the evenings, sometimes together, sometimes alone. On a solo ride he had a flat and did not have what he needed to fix it. He called me to pick him up. I arrived just as the police pulled up. They said nothing, but I assumed it wasn't a coincidence. A tall, imposing African man in an all-white neighborhood most likely had the police called on him.

White supremacy was very much present at Taylor during my college days. I double dated with two friends, a mixed-race couple. One evening, the Black man came to the dorm room visibly shaken, to speak with Bob and me. He was holding in his hand an anonymous letter that he had received from another student warning him that mixed-race dating violated God's law. It was the early 1980s. Bob Jones University had filed suit in 1975 against the IRS for enforcing the Supreme Court decision of 1971, *Green v. Connally*, that refused government funding for educational institutions that violated the 1964 Civil Rights Act because they forbade racially mixed dating. The Reagan administration sided with Bob Jones. The lawyers for Bob Jones University argued the case before the Supreme Court in 1982, the year I graduated from Taylor. The Religious Right emerged in the US from this incident, worried that the government interfered with their religious liberty to enforce what they understood as a biblical mandate. Taylor University had no such rules, but such sentiments were not unusual among evangelicals and Midwesterners in the late seventies and early eighties. We have seen that lingering legacy reignite in the political crises since 2016.

We were not allowed to dance, drink, gamble, or smoke at Taylor University. A high school friend of mine sent me one playing card at a time in letters as a joke, as if he were smuggling in contraband. Bob, one of the gentlest persons that I have known, was expelled for one semester for streaking through a girl's dorm in his underwear, a harmless prank. But on this racist incident, there was no investigation, no expulsions. I should have known at that point that something was deeply off about white, evangelical Christianity in the US. I did not know about the strong opposition in some evangelical quarters to the Civil Rights Act of 1964, or the idea that it was somehow a threat to so-called religious freedom. I was living in a Christian evangelical bubble in the middle of Indiana, singing choruses, raising hands in prayer, riding my bicycle, and ignoring the gross violations of humanity around me. It would take decades before I realized how off, and quite frankly soulless, that kind of Christianity can be. But friendship with Bob keeps me from abandoning it completely.

THE REDEEMING GRACE OF FRIENDSHIP

Bob and I met at Taylor, a conservative, Christian evangelical school set in the middle of cornfields in Indiana. Students describe it by boasting, or lamenting, that there is not a known sin within a ten-mile radius. As the previous section amply testifies, that claim is false. Despite the fact that I had only attended mainline United Methodist churches, I had entered Taylor as a professed evangelical called to be a medical missionary in some remote foreign territory. If entering the priesthood or a religious order confronts young, devout Catholics with the ultimate sacrifice to follow Christ into a life of perfection, being a missionary confronted evangelical Protestants of my generation. We were brought up on stories of Jim Elliott and other missionaries of the 1950s to Ecuador, where they had given up their lives to evangelize the Quechua people. When attacked, they refused to use violence to defend themselves but died demonstrating their faithfulness to the way of the cross. The good questions that have since been raised about the justice or appropriateness of such work had not yet been raised or at least not to or by us. Missionaries regularly came through Taylor University in those days, filling us with stories of martyrdom and glory. In my mind, no greater vocation was possible for a young Christian man. But we were also told that proclaiming the gospel without deeds was the main reason Christianity failed. The gospel had to be lived and proclaimed if it were to be effective. I decided the best way to do that was by becoming a medical doctor and starting a clinic in a foreign place where the gospel was needed. I became a chemistry major and began to study, or at least began to think about studying. My first year in college I did not get much past "beginning" because I spent most of my time running.

My senior year in college was unbearable. I was tired of school, unsure of next steps, and ready to move out of rural Indiana. I wanted adventure. Because I had enough credits to graduate, I worked out an independent study and arranged a semester abroad in Haiti, working in a medical clinic. I escaped, fleeing to what seemed to me to be a desert; it was redeeming but troubling. I had never lived outside Indiana. I had never flown on a plane. Here I was in the north of Haiti observing untold poverty and suffering. It was also the longest stretch in my life without running or cycling on a regular basis. I discovered a great deal about myself in those four months, and the first was that I had little to offer the people in Haiti. I had not thought deeply enough about what it meant to be a missionary.

My first day in Haiti, I went for a walk along a creek when a thin, gaunt man approached me with outstretched hand, shouting, "Ban mwen dolla, Ban mwen dolla." I did not yet know any Creole, but I understood he was asking for money. I had nothing to give him and no way of explaining it. I put my palms out to signify that I had nothing, only to be confronted more insistently, "Ban mwen dolla!" It was devastating and revealing at the same time. I went back to my solitary room and wondered what I had done. Why was I here, another mouth to feed in a country with too many hungry people? I had no useful skills, no facility with the language, and little cross-cultural awareness. There were more than sufficient numbers of

Haitian preachers and teachers; I was not needed for that. I was useless. I spent the next four months working alongside people with whom I could barely communicate on construction projects, hauling blocks, mixing mud, and laying brick.

I took at least three things away from that experience. First was the uncomfortable solitude that forced contemplation. New questions arose about faith, life, and vocation as I witnessed poverty even deeper than I had seen in Buffalo. Second was the overwhelming generosity and hospitality of the Haitian people. I had nothing to offer, but they took me in without resentment. Third was the music. I would return from the construction site on a truck full of Haitian coworkers singing spirituals that opened up heaven. When I hear calls to build a wall along our southern border and keep undesirables out, when I see desperate families from whom children have been separated from their parents and placed in detention campus, when I see signs stating, "America First!," I cannot help but hear that music, remember that hospitality, and wonder how the world became so out of joint that the poor almost always seem ready to welcome the rich but we the rich seldom return the favor. When I see members of the Christian faith joining in these sentiments, I wonder if Christianity in the US has become so corrupt that it is beyond redemption. Then I remember my college roommate and running and cycling partner, Bob. If I did not know people like him, I might despair of Christianity.

Bob and Steve in 2019 after forty years of friendship.

Returning to Indiana and graduation at Taylor, I was wiser but more confused than when I left. I wanted to discuss with everyone what I had witnessed and learned, but the busyness of life always gets in the way. There is seldom time for adequate reflection. Graduation exercises and parties, plans for what happens next, moving out of the dorm, and saying goodbyes left little time to debrief, except with Bob. He was there as a good friend listening and helping me make sense of my experiences. He had been my roommate for three years and in that time we became best friends. We first met during our freshman year at the preseason cross-country team's training camp and became immediate friends and have been so since despite our paths going in different directions. Bob headed more deeply into the best of evangelical Christianity and I headed out of it to a more ecumenical and mainline form of Christianity. He worked and lived in majority communities of poverty, primarily Black and brown. He raised his children in difficult areas of the US, often in places controlled by gangs. He has been beaten, intimidated, embraced, and served as a refuge for many. He works in children and teen ministry, often with the children or relatives of gang members and teens headed into or out of gangs. He lived and worked for a time in a home that assisted gang members exiting their previous life by fleeing the areas where becoming a member of a gang was often the only way to survive. The home was a refuge where they could live for several years as they took on their new life in faith. He worked for the redemption of men whose life had been derailed by gang violence, both perpetrated against and by them.

I have lived my life in university settings. I've never been physically threatened, except for the occasional empty threat from angry motorists, much less beaten up. A typical conversation with Bob begins like this: "Well the first time I got beaten up was when we lived in the 'devil's half mile,' otherwise known as 'Belmont triangle' because people entered into it and never came out." Bob was told by gang members that his house was the safest on the block because the gangs protected it. Because he built friendships with and among gang members, they trusted him and encouraged their youth to attend his center. Many hoped that their children, nephews, nieces, and friends might escape the life they found necessary for survival.

The safest house, however, did not mean one absolutely secure from violence. At one teen meeting, rival gangs began fighting in the parking lot of the teen center. Bob was frustrated because the center was supposed to be a safe zone. He stands five foot nine inches and weighs about one hundred and forty pounds. He has the slender shape of a runner, the result of having run all his life. He is fit but not intimidating. He also has one of the kindest dispositions of anyone that I have ever known. He does not get rattled or angered easily. His college nickname was "Nice Guy Bob." On this occasion he was unhappy. The gang members had violated the sanctity of the teen center. Upset, he grabbed one, a person who is currently in prison serving a sentence for a triple homicide, in an attempt to separate the fighting factions. The person did not turn on Bob, but Bob happened to grab him just as a rival gang member squared up to throw a punch with the full force of his body. The fellow Bob grabbed saw the punch coming and ducked, bringing Bob's face into direct contact with the rival member's fist. He hit Bob squarely in the side of the face, knocking him to the ground. Bob later realized that a person behind him was holding a knife and had the punch knocked him in the center of his face, the force could have pushed him back into the knife. Bob was uncharacteristically angry. He pulled himself up from the ground and began yelling at the fighting gang members. They were so startled at his reaction that they ceased their fighting, parted from each other, and went away. As a minister, Bob has buried at least a half dozen of those gang members.

Guns were strictly forbidden in the center, but Lucky, a teen who attended one of Bob's meetings, concealed his uncle's gun. During the evening meeting, Lucky was pelted with candy corn thrown by another teen who intended to provoke him. "Who the hell did that?" he yelled as he pulled out a gun and began waving it around. The other teens hit the ground. Bob told the other staff to get the fellow who threw the candy corn out of the room as he ran toward Lucky. Bob told me that he learned to get directly in the face of the teens when they were threatening violence to break eye contact with the person with whom they were in an altercation. Once they lost sight of the person inciting their wrath, the anger would diminish. It worked with Lucky. Bob then told Lucky to give him the gun so he could discard it. Lucky told him that it was his uncle's, and he would be beaten if he lost it. Bob told him he at least had to hide it and never bring it into the center if he wanted to attend the meeting. Lucky left the room, hid the gun, and returned.

Bob has befriended "OGs," the "original gangsters" who made up the Crips and the Bloods in Los Angeles. He has not hesitated to put himself in harm's way and has done so without ever possessing or owning a gun himself. This never kept him from exhibiting a charitable courage. He was driving with his wife through a gang-controlled area to visit friends and witnessed a man by the side of the road whose hands were on a woman's throat, obviously intending serious harm. Bob could see the fear in her eyes. He stopped his car, got out, and confronted the man. He was uncertain if the man spoke English, but he wanted to question his actions and make sure he understood. Bob's Spanish was too spotty so he asked a bystander to translate for him, saying, "You should not be doing this. How can I pray for you?" The potential translator responded, "Are you sure you want to tell him that?" Bob affirmed it, and the translator conveyed Bob's message. The violent man did not appreciate it. He turned toward Bob, letting go of the woman long enough so that she could scramble away. Then the man said to Bob in perfect English, "I'm going to kick your mother-fucking ass." He made good on his promise, knocking Bob to the ground and pummeling him with his boots. When Bob told me this story, he had his characteristic smile and said, "You know what upset me the most was that he stepped on my new sunglasses and broke them." We both laughed at the absurdity. Lying on the ground, Bob responded to his beating by telling the man, "What's your problem? You need Jesus." He was embarrassed that he had been so soundly beaten in front of his wife, even as he recognizes that such a macho sentiment is far from Christian virtue.

The philosopher Friedrich Nietzsche said that there has only been one Christian on the earth, and he died on the cross. Most days, I am tempted to think Nietzsche correct. Many of us who claim Christian faith are practical atheists; it makes little difference for how we live and there is little evidence that we have taken up any cross and followed Christ. Some who take the name use it primarily to dominate others. The well-known German theologian Dietrich Bonhoeffer, who died at the hands of the Nazis for his resistance, once wrote, "When Christ bids someone come and follow, he bids them come and die." That death is seldom a literal death, but there can be no true Christian faith without letting go of some worldly hindrance such as wealth, greed, hatred, prestige, power, racism, misogyny, the desire to dominate others, white supremacy, and so on. Bob's life proves Nietzsche wrong.

Despite our close friendship, Bob's life and mine went in different directions. He will tell me, "You know, Steve, I was praying and the Lord said to me . . ." My academic training causes me to pause before such language and ask questions like, "Under what conditions could we say that the Lord speaks to you?" I'm skeptical of such language, especially when it is used by lives marked by practical atheism. John Wesley, the eighteenth-century reformer and evangelist and founder of the Methodists, once wrote that there are few Christians upon the face of the earth, and they are seldom found in places where you would think to look for them. I agree and have grown suspicious of most claims Christians make, especially after the mirror that Trumpism has held up to us that exposed Christianity, especially white, evangelical Christianity, for what it is. That vision cannot be unseen. Evangelical language is not alien to me. I'm accustomed to it, and once found myself at home in it. It has become more alien and can even make me cringe. But when Bob uses it, I still listen.

3

The Broken Middle

We only know the beginning from the middle. We find ourselves in the middle of things before we are able to understand their origin. The origin has a mysteriousness that we can never fully comprehend. We trace effects back to causes and are often unable to name those causes well. This child came from these parents who came from those and so on. This political society came from these historical developments. These mountain ranges rose up from those previous geological transformations. These virtues or vices were given rise to by these forms of life. Despite our best efforts, the origins maintain an element of incompleteness. We work backwards from what we have before us to what we conceive its origin to be. Perhaps this is why Aristotle's argument for the eternality of the universe puzzled Medieval theologians. Can we know the origin of something so vast? It seemed reasonable to conceive of it without beginning. If every effect had a cause except God, who was the self-caused cause, was it possible that there might be other effects that lacked a singular cause? Perhaps the universe was not laid out linearly but cyclically, repeating itself non-identically with no origin, only the constant movement from potentiality to actuality, its dissipation back to potentiality, and reconfiguration into new and emergent actualities? We are in the middle, trying to make sense of our beginnings; to do so has an irreducible element of faith that what we can see makes sense because of what we cannot see, which is as true of an individual life as it is of the universe. The middle is always broken, cut off from its beginning and yet rendered intelligible by it. Through faith and hope, we are able to see the origin as a gift.

FRACTURES, WOUNDS, AND LIVING WELL

When I learned to play basketball, I never imagined it would lead to years of long-distance running. Had basketball worked out, long-distance running would not have become an obsession. Had running not been taken away, cycling would not have replaced it. Like many good things in life, the joy from decades of long-distance cycling came about by accident; it was a gift, albeit a strange one. Human beings become unstable when they sit atop two wheels. Add speed to that instability and tragedy is inevitable. Anyone who regularly rides a bicycle will crash. Crashing hurts. The preferred way to do it is to slide along the pavement and lose clothing and skin, causing "road rash," rather than going straight into the road and breaking bones. Once the dirt of road rash is cleaned out and Tegaderm applied, it will heal in a week or so. Broken bones take longer.

I have not kept track of all my crashes over the years, but I assume I have averaged one or two per year, most inconsequential, some spectacular. I've broken my collar bone three times, bones in both my hands, and two ribs. As noted, fractures most often occur when the body goes straight into the pavement rather than skimming along it. The day my daughter went into labor with our first granddaughter, Harper, I had a high-speed crash on the South Loop that left me with a broken helmet, a slight concussion, and the worst road rash of my life—but no broken bones. I was in bad shape but decided to ride home slowly. A good cycling friend insisted that he accompany me. We never made it home. I was getting woozy and he thought it best to pull into a parking lot and call Ricka. Patrick guided me into the parking lot, sat me down, and figured out how to call my wife on my phone. The next thing I remember was Ricka picking me up with the car in the Osco parking lot. I later had only the slightest memory of it. Ricka picked me up, cleaned out the wounds, applied the all-too-familiar Tegaderm, and then observed me over the next several hours to make sure I did not fall asleep, following standard concussion protocols. That evening the phone rang, informing us that our daughter had gone into labor; she was two weeks early. Ricka promised that she would be there for the delivery. We had a standby flight reserved. She looked at me and said, "You have no choice but to be okay because I'm going to Chicago to help with the birth." I assured her that I would be fine, and she took off for the airport.

I've had so many crashes and fractures that I have had friends who, out of genuine concern, questioned why I continue to ride. I replied that recovering from broken bones was better than heart disease, thinking my cycling would ward off the latter even if it brought on the former. (That now seems ironic.) It takes six weeks to recover from broken bones; it is possible to ride indoors much sooner than that, but breaking bones takes its toll. The third time I broke my collar bone I was despondent and frustrated, wondering if cycling was worth it. Ricka picked me up and drove me to the hospital. On the way to the hospital, I said to her, "Do you want me to give this up?" Without hesitating she responded, "I don't want to live with you if you do."

Was it a mistake not giving up cycling? I think not and have no regrets. Every bicycle ride is a reminder of the fragility of life, of its tendency toward dissolution. Everything gets fractured. A person is born into fractured relations in their family, neighborhood, society, the church, and more. Bone fractures heal. These other fractures can be more persistent. To live well is not to avoid the fractures but to recognize them and seek their healing. To live well is also to learn to die well, and that entails asking, "What is a life worth living?" Whatever it is, it will not come about if we attempt to protect it from risk with a secure plan that avoids all fractures.

Family, society, politics, and the church bear the wounds of fracture and division. Anyone who ignores those wounds, denies division, and fails to attend to the conditions for their possible healing, cannot live well. Healing, of course, takes time, and usually does not occur without pain. The pain is not an end in itself, it exists for the sake of healing. The scars I bear on my back and hip are a reminder, like the scars for my pacemakers, that healing and wholeness can be difficult, and yet are also the results of healing surgeries. Without challenging misogyny, white supremacy, ecclesial divisions, vast economic inequality, there can be no wholeness. The wounds we inherit cannot be sources for healing if they go unacknowledged; then they only fester. Wounds in themselves, of course, are neither healing nor redemptive. Some wounds are so deep that you wonder if healing can occur this side of the eschaton. How does one make sense of the wounds from the genocide of Indigenous Americans, American slavery, the Holocaust, the Irish famines, from deep family traumas, from natural evils like tsunamis and so much more? Wounds can be deep, general, and historical with lingering effects. They are also specific and personal. It would be better if we did not have them, but healing depends not on whether life gets fractured but how we receive the brokenness. Just as the wounds of Christ are the font of the sacraments, so our wounds can be life-giving rather than death-dealing. For that, they need to be something more than mere wounds.

The first profound wound I witnessed came at the age of fifteen. My father had been fired as principal of the local high school. Because of his admirable reputation, he quickly found a new position. We were moving from Knox to Wabash, Indiana and a few friends had a going-away party for me. Two of them had motorcycles, one of them brand new. Although none of us had licenses (we were only fifteen), we decided to race through our small town. I wanted to ride on the new bike and tried to get on it, but another had already called it and I was delegated to the back seat of the older, slower bike. We were racing on a rural road, riding neck and neck when the faster bike began pulling away. We came to a stop sign and our motorcycle slowed down, but the other driver decided to gain advantage by running the stop sign. He did not see the car coming his way; it hit them square on. It was the most horrifying thing that I had witnessed to that point in my life. The car crumpled. The motorcycle busted into pieces. Metal splashed like a diver landing in water. Just as a diver disappears into the water, one of my friends disappeared within the wreckage. The other flew more than twenty feet in our direction; we watched him pass by, coming to rest, crumpled and unmoving, in a field.

Fifty-five years later, I still vividly recall that accident. The fabric of life was torn, and a gaping wound emerged that was filled with death. Convinced both of my friends were dead and frightened to look upon them, I jumped off the motorcycle and began running toward the local hospital, approximately one mile away. For some reason I knew that they would be brought there, and thought it was where I should wait for the news whether they were dead or alive. Once at the hospital, I spent the time on my knees praying. Never in my life had I prayed like that. They arrived at the hospital alive, but in critical condition. One was in a coma for months; the other had multiple fractures that required a lengthy hospital stay. Their lives were changed forever, at a young age. Although I have ridden bicycles since then, I cannot get on a motorcycle without reliving that moment. I know it makes no sense. I've ridden a bicycle through the Rocky Mountains on an interstate highway through tunnels, but I would not ride a motorcycle in my neighborhood.

If wounds are sources for healing, those sources are something other than the wounds themselves. Suffering in itself is not redemptive. It hurts. If possible, it should be avoided. Christ's sufferings on the cross were not something he embraced without fear. They were neither what he nor the Father directly willed. As St. Anselm put it, what God willed as Father, Son, and Spirit, was the Son's obedience to the goodness God created and humanity wounded. Because of his perfect obedience, Jesus was willing to give himself over passively and indirectly to those wounds, to be crucified, killed, and handed over to others who would lay his dead body in the tomb. All this was our doing, a sign of our unwillingness to recognize inflicting wounds on others for what it is, a sign of fallenness. God, who is the good, comes among us and we are threatened. We wound, thinking death might secure our existence, only to discover that it is not in wounding, but in the wound's overcoming that we are healed. Life, not suffering and death, is God's will. Jesus is risen from the dead. He bears the wounds, but it is in their healing that we too are healed.

BODILY FRACTURES

No one gets through life without some wounds; our bodies bear their marks. Occasions arise when we give ourselves over to anticipated but unsettling wounding such as surgery or rehabilitation. Drugs like Versed and fentanyl take off the edge before giving a surgeon permission to slice open the body, even if it is for one's good. Most wounds, however, take us by surprise; we do not see them coming. My first major bicycle accident took place in 1985 in a road race, the Tour de Moore in Southern Pines, North Carolina. The Tour de Moore began in 1976 and had a thirty-nine-year history before it ended. On April 17, 2015 the local newspaper, *The Pilot*, ran a column declaring the race's obituary, noting, "the race over the years survived spectacular crashes." Mine was not the most spectacular. In 1991 a car crested a hill and came upon the peloton during the race. It surprised the driver, who hit the brakes, lost control, and slid into the riders, taking out more than forty of them. Eighteen riders were taken to Moore Regional Hospital; thankfully, no one was killed. In the 1985 crash, only one person was taken to Moore Regional Hospital, who happened to be me. For the first quarter century of my life, I had never broken a bone. The Tour de Moore introduced me to bodily fractures.

The Tour de Moore suited my cycling abilities. It was a longer road race with some elevation. Most bicycle races are criteriums. They are spectator friendly and easy to control. In a criterium, a city blocks off a four-square area about one mile in length and racers speed around the blocked off area in a more or less full-out sprint. Spectators can watch the race unfold from a single observation point. The key to racing well in a criterium is to get to the front early and stay there as long as you can. If a rider gets caught in the back of the peloton, they will experience a slingshot effect, slowing into the corners as the riders bunch up, and sprinting out of them, putting out as much power as possible in the straightaway as the bunched riders race to hang on to the peloton. The lead riders do not need to slow down as much and can ride at a more even pace. To get to the front a rider must go full out into the corners, taking them as fast as possible, and maintaining speed as long as possible. Every other cyclist has the same idea, but physics will not accommodate everyone going into the corner at the same time with the same speed. It has the feeling of a game of chicken. Whoever concedes the corner to another rider most likely loses.

I was insufficiently powerful and overly cautious to do well in criteriums. I entered fewer than ten in my limited time racing and much preferred longer road races. Except for the occasional breakaway or acceleration up a hill, the pace in a road race was more consistent than the surging and sprinting in a crit, but road races are more difficult to find. They are not as easily controlled, and spectators cannot watch the race unfold, so sponsors prefer criteriums.

The Tour de Moore was one of the few road races available. The race began well enough for me. I was in the main peloton and could see the lead riders at the front. We had been told to stay to the right of the yellow lane or risk disqualification, because the road remained open to automobiles. We were bunched closely together, riding side by side from the right of the road to the yellow line with little chance of advancing position this early in the race. A group of five riders decided to violate the rules and ride to the left of the yellow lane, the only place possible to make progress. The peloton became jumpy as other riders watched them pass, moving toward the front. The key to riding safely in a peloton is not to make sudden moves and to maintain one's line, that is, to stay directly behind the person in front of you until the race opens up and you can safely move up. We were riding along at twenty-five-plus mph when a rider two or three ahead of me decided he would force his way to the left edge and grab onto the five cheating riders who were riding outside the yellow. There was no space for him to do so and he caught a rider to his left by surprise. They touched wheels and riders fell like dominos; carnage ensued. Fifteen to twenty cyclists went head over heels into the road. I was right in the middle of the felled cyclists, going straight over the handlebars and into the road. A searing pain ripped through my right shoulder.

Despite having ridden for five years and having had a few minor crashes, I never experienced anything like this and had no idea what this strange feeling was. I knew something was wrong. What was it, this new and confusing feeling? I pulled myself to the side of the road and nearly fainted from the pain. A fellow crashed cyclist saw my discomfort and the color disappearing from my face. He took off my helmet and encouraged me to put my head between my knees. My color returned. The ambulance arrived; medics triaged the situation and determined that I was the only one who had broken anything. I experienced my first ambulance ride to the hospital and first broken collar bone.

Over the next few years, Ricka gave birth to our daughter Lindsey in 1986 and Rebecca in 1989. Shortly after Rebecca was born, four years after the first broken collar bone, I was out on a solo training ride doing hill work: sprinting up one side of a hill, coasting down the next, repeating. Arriving at the top of a hill, I heard a noise and looked left just in time to see a woman opening the pen that held her large German shepherd. Before she could leash him, he saw me and took off at full velocity. Panicked, I decided to try to outrun him. I started down the hill attempting to gain speed, but it was too late; with a perfect angle, he had the drop on me and was steadily gaining ground. I pedaled faster. He accelerated. I started yelling. He barked louder. Now he was upon me and I knew it was going to hurt. I've been chased by dogs many times but never with this ferocity and recklessness; they usually back off when you yell at them. This dog was single minded, but rather than attacking me he lunged onto my front wheel, catapulting me into the road and momentarily knocking himself out. When he came to, he walked away whimpering.

I lay on the pavement writhing in pain. This time there was no confusion as to what had happened. The searing pain that visited my right shoulder in 1985 was now doing the same to the left. At least I was not confused. The woman who owned the dog apologized and asked me if I was okay. I told her my collar bone was broken. She called a sheriff, who arrived and called an ambulance. The sheriff took my information and told me that he would let my wife know what happened. I said to him, "Let her know I'm okay. It is another broken collar bone." He went to our house, knocked on the door, and told her that I had been in an accident and was in the ER at Duke University Hospital. He neglected to convey my soothing message. Ricka found it odd that a sheriff had come to the house and assumed the worst. She imagined that I must be in serious condition. She gathered Lindsey and Rebecca and beelined for the ER, wanting the kids to have the opportunity to say goodbye if it was necessary. She worked at Duke Hospital, so when they forbade her from taking the children into the ER, she ignored them and immediately entered with two little girls in tow, searching among the patients to find me. Hospitals and doctors never intimidate her like they do me. She found me lying on a wood gurney being checked out to make sure it was nothing more than a collar bone. I told Ricka what had happened, and Lindsey, three years old, looked up with a deeply troubled expression that warmed my heart because of her concern. Then she asked, "Dad, Dad, how is the dog? Is the dog okay?" Our family recites that story, laughing every time we recall it.

PRAYERFUL INTERLUDE

The second time I broke my collar bone, Rebecca was still in the crib. I was in graduate school, working on my dissertation, and Ricka was working weekends on the oncology unit at Duke Hospital. With my broken collar bone, I could barely lift Rebecca in and out of the crib. My good friend Fritz Bauerschmidt would come over on the weekends to help with Becky, lifting her out and putting her back in the crib. He was part of a prayer group that developed while we were in graduate school. Our mutual friend, John Berkman, suggested to several of us that prayer should be an essential piece of our graduate theological training. Graduate school consumes time and energy such that the most important matters, like prayer and family, easily get neglected. A few graduate students agreed with John and we began to meet weekly for prayer. Originally, we were unsuccessful, tending to discuss theology, philosophy, and our classwork more than praying. We expanded our group, adding spouses and friends, who helped us avoid insider theological discussions and kept us focused on prayer.

Our prayer group was half Protestant and half Catholic. Many of the Catholics had been involved in the Jesuit Volunteer Corps. I had never heard of it but quickly became impressed with the people in the prayer group who had gone through it. Some of today's leading theologians were members of that prayer group. Along with Fritz and John, Michael Baxter, Dan Bell, William Cavanaugh, Jim Fodor, David McCarthy, and David Jenkins were members. David Jenkins is a fellow Methodist pastor who taught me to love the Eucharist. As a campus minister at Duke, he invited me to preside weekly for the undergraduate population. My bishop ordained me, but it was David who confirmed my vocation to the ministry. Because we were half Catholic and Protestant, we knew it would be controversial for the prayer group to share the Eucharist. We discovered other ways to participate in the life of each other's church as much as we could, but a desire for the unity of the church that would permit full communion welled up in me from the years spent in prayer with such good people.

The theologians were a majority male group and that brought its own set of problems. Fortunately, friends and family members supplemented us: Ricka, Maureen Sweeney, Tracy Rowan, Holly Jones, Janine Crawley, Bridgett McCarthy, and others. Some of them were former Jesuit Volunteer Corps (JVC) members who moved to Durham; others were Methodists who had gone through seminary and were still in the area. Still others were seekers who had become disenfranchised from their local churches. Some of them moved in together and established "Iredell House" in an attempt to live in community.

Ricka and I were members of the prayer group for seven years. The first few years it met in our home because we were the only ones who had young children; we met on Sunday evening after they were asleep. Fritz and Maureen then had children and we would meet in their home. Iredell House lasted long past our time. Both Mike Baxter and I taught master's degree students who went to Duke for their doctoral work and lived there. The friendships made in that prayer group have had lasting effects. We remained close over the years, attending baptisms, weddings, and other joyous occasions. We have not yet had funerals. When Maureen heard about my cardiac failure she wrote and said, "Stop it, Steve. You are making us feel old."

When our daughter Rebecca wanted to spend one year between undergraduate and graduate school doing nonprofit work, I encouraged her to consider JVC. Because we were not Catholic, she was skeptical. After looking into it, she thought it might be a fit, applied, and was accepted. Her year in JVC was deeply formative. It is where she met her Adam. When our prayer group formed, she was still in her crib and now those friendships bore fruit in her life without her even knowing all that had gone into it. Subsequently, she became Roman Catholic.

Our prayer group not only prayed, but also became involved in common projects. Maureen is a well-known professor at the University of Maryland Francis King Carey School of Law, specializing in immigration law. When we first met, she was an immigration rights advocate for migrant workers in North Carolina. She would inform us of the plight of seasonal farm workers, and we would pray for them. Prayer requires more than well-wishing, of course. She came to us on one occasion with an urgent request. A young Guatemalan girl from the Maya highlands had a baby. I was aware of the terrible political situation in the Maya highlands from time living in Honduras. Aid workers had told us stories of the indiscriminate warfare against supposed communist insurgents that resulted in mass civilian casualties.

I don't know if Juana escaped that specific situation, but for some reason she was sent via a coyote (a person who for a fee illegally brings people to the US) to work the fields. She did not know how old she was, but she could not have been more than fifteen or sixteen. Somewhere along the way she had been raped and had given birth to her son in the fields on a day when she was working. The man who raped her wanted to take the baby from her and she needed protection. Juana spoke no English and only a little Spanish. Her main language was a Mayan dialect. Maureen knew that Ricka spoke fluent Spanish and that someone was always home during the day at our house because we arranged our schedule so that one of us was there with the children. She asked if we could watch Juana and her newborn son during the day while they stayed with her and Fritz during the evening.

For several months, Juana stayed with us and her son shared a crib with our Becky. Juana was at that time undocumented; she has since become a US citizen. I was told at the time that it was not illegal to take an undocumented person into your house, but it was illegal to transport them. I don't know what the law is now. I do know that Christians should take seriously their vocation to be hospitable, especially to those who are the "least" among us. In providing food and shelter to them, we do nothing less than provide it to Christ. How do so many US Christians decide that citizenship and national boundaries take precedence over the bonds of baptism? Why are so many afraid of people like Juana? She was no threat. No one wanted her job, and she did not take one from anyone. Her low wages made possible the cheap fruits and vegetables we enjoy year-round. I don't know how any person of faith could have said no to her, given her plight.

Raising children is time-consuming, joyful, and exhausting. I was in the worst physical condition of my life when the children were young. I took care of them Friday-Sunday when Ricka worked and she did so Monday-Thursday when I did. Riding created tension back then. We were so busy; it was an unnecessary luxury. On the few occasions Ricka had a weekend off, I might get out for a short ride. On occasion she would ask, "Do you really need to ride today?" Once our children were grown and out of the house, things changed. I rode much more and she grew so accustomed to her leisurely Saturday mornings alone during my long rides that if she woke and found me home, she would say, "Why are you not out riding your bike?"

Twenty-two years passed between my second and third catastrophic crashes. Twenty-two years of cycling without a significant crash is an achievement. We left Durham for King of Prussia, Pennsylvania in 1995, and bought a house along the Schuylkill River. A paved bicycle trail follows the Schuylkill into Philadelphia, where I became a faculty member at the Jesuit University, St. Joseph's. It was fifteen miles from my door to my office, all but the last two on the bicycle trail. Anyone who has driven along the "Schuylkill Expressway" (I-76) into Philly knows that it is a nightmare. Stuck between the river to the east and hills to the west, it has insufficient space for the volume of traffic and resembles a parking lot more than an expressway. I could bike the fifteen miles to St. Joseph's as quick as driving the stressful expressway. Our children were small, so commuting by bicycle took no time away from them. I had a few minor crashes during those years, but nothing serious.

In 1998 we moved to Skokie, Illinois when I became assistant professor of systematic theology at Garrett-Evangelical Theological Seminary, on the campus of Northwestern University. I had been a cycling commuter for a decade by then and knew to look for a home that would make for a safe and convenient commute to the office. We bought a house next to a bicycle trail along the North Branch Trail in the Cook County Forest Preserve. Although I only lived four miles from work, I could take the trail, ride seven and one-half miles north, get on safe roads going south, have a safe commute into Northwestern, and reach my daily thirty-mile goal.

VOCATIONAL AND ECCLESIAL FRACTURES

The Chicago metroplex was the most congested place I ever lived. The forest preserve was an oasis, filled with deer, rabbits, coyotes, and the occasional fox. The seminary was not a good fit for me. At the faculty retreat my first semester, lunching with other faculty members whom I did not yet know well, one turned to me and said, "I hear you are part of the right-wing take-over of the seminary." Stunned, I did not know how to respond. I mumbled something along the lines, "Well, that comes as a surprise to me." The first few years I attempted to dissuade the senior faculty, to no avail, that I was not who some thought I was. Eventually, I gave up and frequently said pro-vocative things in faculty meetings that confirmed their suspicions. It was liberating to fail in my endeavor to be included in the dominant faculty consensus and I wondered why it had mattered to me in the first place. The provocations were, however, unnecessary and I learned from my significant failures from those days how to be a better colleague when joining other faculties. I made some very good friends on faculty at Garrett, and had some excellent students, and that sufficed to make work worthwhile, but it was not easy to work in an environment where I felt distrusted. The thirty-mile daily commute allowed me to clear my head and gain perspective.

After nearly a decade working in that environment, I knew it was time to leave Garrett and began to apply for other positions. Despite my later awareness of the problem of white supremacy within evangelical Christian-ity, I thought I could find a place within it and often sought to address an evangelical audience in my theological work. I had positive experiences at Taylor University and knew beautiful, faithful people like Bob. White su-premacy was very much alive, but Taylor was by no means defined only by that doctrine; evangelical Christianity is not purely evil, as if anything could be. Taylor was named after Bishop William Taylor, a missionary bishop in the Methodist-Episcopal Church in the mid-nineteenth century. As an or-dained Methodist elder, I found that the Wesleyan evangelical Christianity that formed Bishop Taylor continued to linger at Taylor University, and it enriched my own faith and vocation.

I only visited Taylor a few times since graduating in 1982. I was invited back in 2016 to be part of a discussion on education in a theological context for the inauguration of Taylor's thirty-first president. I was surprised at how alien the place had become; it was a surprise because despite the racist incident, I had had good experiences at Taylor. I raised a few questions to the faculty and students assembled for the panel discussion in 2016, questions that I had learned during my time at Taylor. Should we be willing to use violence in either service to the nation-state or protection of our own property? Should we submit to the rampant gun culture of the United States and arm ourselves? How shall we live with our possessions, our property, money, and economic privileges? I suggested that these questions were much more pressing than some of the concerns present in Taylor's "Life Together Covenant." For instance, it expresses its opposition to smoking, alcohol, gambling, and dancing, and emphasizes "submission to civil authority," citing Romans 13:1. Yet it neglects another clear strand of biblical teaching that requires us to challenge unjust civil authority found in passages like Revelation 13 and elsewhere. Given this emphasis in its "Life Together Covenant" on submission to authority, it came as no surprise that Taylor invited the controversial Vice President Mike Pence, whom conservative columnist George Will referred to as "the worst person in government" because of his "toadyism," to give the 2019 commencement address. Many Taylor alums spoke out against it, sending letters to the president and board of trustees. I joined them out of a deep worry that Taylor was traveling the same road of the irreparably compromised Liberty University.

Perhaps my memory is kind, but I think evangelical culture shifted from my time at Taylor in the late 1970s to 2016. Perhaps it was Ronald Reagan's successful co-optation of evangelical Christianity for a culture war project in the 1980s? Perhaps the shift was less than I remember, and I was not paying attention? After all, Phyllis Schlafly was the "women's week" speaker when I was a student. I certainly moved in a different theological direction after Taylor, first working with a devoted liberation Methodist theologian in Honduras and then doing a Master's and PhD at Duke University under the mentorship of Stanley Hauerwas, the well-known pacifist theologian.

Hauerwas was influenced by the Mennonite theologian John Howard Yoder. Though both have influenced my own work in Christian nonviolence, I was first challenged with a Christian's attitude toward peace and violence at Taylor University when my physical chemistry professor asked our class to read Senator Mark Hatfield's 1977 work *Between a Rock and a Hard Place*, explaining his opposition to the Vietnam War. I did not find out Hatfield had been influenced by Yoder for another thirty years. I did not know who Yoder was when I read Hatfield's book, but it made a strong impression on me. I remember discussing the issues that he raised late into the night with Taylor friends. It was through those conversations that my later concerns with war, policing, domestic abuse, sexual harassment, torture, racism, mass incarceration, solitary confinement, and unjust economic relations first germinated. I owe students and faculty at Taylor a debt of gratitude for first drawing my attention to these issues.

Questions of wealth and poverty were more prevalent during my time at Taylor than ones about homosexuality. It should be noted that there are only seven passages on homosexuality in both the Old Testament and New Testament, but there are thousands about the use of money. Why are the former so visible as an issue within contemporary evangelical churches and the latter invisible? Don't get me wrong, discussing sexuality is important. Sex matters, but it is a minor issue in Scripture compared to economics. Perhaps faithful relations with others require more intentionality, being concerned with how we make our money by not profiting off the suffering of others, by what we do with it, and by how much we keep? Perhaps we should commit ourselves to a maximum moral income, thus holding ourselves accountable to living on no more than $150,000, $200,000, or $250,000, with everything else going to the poor? It was precisely because I met and continue to know people from Taylor who have lived admirable, faithful lives that I do not regret my time there. I am no fan of large, independent, evangelical megachurches and think Christianity in the US would be much better without them, but admirable evangelical communities can still be found, albeit seldom on television.

In all events, my life has not been spent among evangelicals. After leaving Taylor I primarily lived and worked among mainline Protestants, Roman Catholics, and secularists. I now find myself more comfortable in these settings. When I was at Garrett I had been invited to apply for a chair in theology at a premier evangelical college and I needed a change. I went through the lengthy application process, and the theology faculty had been scheduled to vote on my candidacy. Several friends on faculty who had recruited me for the chair thought that I had the votes for the position. It was in proximity to where we were living. If I received the chair, my family would not have to move. My prospects were so promising that I figured out a cycling commute, charting a route, but it was not meant to be. One of the faculty members who thought I was insufficiently evangelical discovered a controversial editorial I had written, "In need of a pope? Protestants and the papacy." They had just fired a faculty member who had converted to

Catholicism and had, and still have, a requirement that Catholics cannot be on faculty. As the faculty department prepared to vote on my candidacy, the president dispatched the provost to inform them that they could not vote because I would not be permitted to teach at their institution given my Catholic sympathies.

So the editorial in which I raised the question, "Do Protestants need the papacy?," torpedoed my candidacy.[6] I wrote it immediately after the death of John Paul II and the election of Benedict XVI. My friend Jason Byassee, an editor for the *Christian Century*, put together an article on Protestant responses to the papacy. He asked me if I could write some kind of affirmation from a Protestant perspective. He needed it soon. I agreed, went out for a run, and composed the editorial in my head while running on the trails in Cook County's Forest Preserve. After the run, I sat down and wrote the editorial in under two hours. I've spent years working on books that only a few people read and even fewer commented on or reviewed. I have no hard data but given the response and the number of times this editorial was cited, favorably and negatively, and given the number of unsolicited emails and comments that I received about it, this editorial may have garnered more responses than anything else I've written.

That I found myself defending Catholicism is a surprise. Catholicism felt odd to me growing up, far removed from the comfortability of mainline Protestant and evangelical Christianity. I experienced Catholicism as ritualistic, authoritarian, clannish, superstitious, and impersonal. One of the gifts in my life is the change that occurred in my attitude toward Catholicism because of many Catholic friends, our collaborations, and the time spent working in two Catholic universities. I went from being suspicious of Catholic theology to being deeply appreciative and profoundly influenced by it. My earlier suspicion of Catholicism was unsurprising for a Protestant. As a tradition of protest, it requires some object to set itself against. That object was often the papacy and for centuries, Protestants considered the pope to be the antichrist. The Orthodox Church has a strain of this as well. It surfaced in 2016 when Pope Francis was greeted in Tbilisi, Georgia with protestors holding signs, "The Pope is the Antichrist."

Given the Protestant history of anti-papal pronouncements, I thought it important to acknowledge in 2005 how much had changed in Protestant-Catholic relations. Don't get me wrong. I have no romantic illusions about the papacy. I grieve over the mishandling of the sexual abuse crisis and lament how many US Catholic bishops, appointed by John Paul II and Benedict XVI, engage in culture warring. Too many Catholic leaders have been inept at providing wisdom during the rise of populist authoritarian governments or the coronavirus pandemic. I am aware of some of the negative aspects of the papacy's historical legacy and the justifiable reasons why Protestants and Catholics separated. But once again we must recognize that Catholics themselves, to some extent, acknowledge this. The Catholic Church has acknowledged contributing to the ruptures that divide us, ruptures that are always sin. We Protestants must now reciprocate and name our sin in dividing Christ's body.

At one point in history, to be a Protestant was explicitly or tacitly to will an end to the papacy. I think many Protestants can now confess that was a mistaken view. Both the church and the world would sorely lack a necessary witness if there were no Pope Francis. This does not require abandoning what is good in Protestant traditions. I for one cannot leave my Wesleyan communion behind. The hymns, doctrine, discipline, and liturgy of that tradition gave me faith and taught me to love God. Nor can I will an end to the unity the papacy clearly produces throughout the world. So, what is to be done? Only two possibilities seem to present themselves. Either we try to find a place for our separated communities from within the Catholic Church or we find a place for catholic unity from within our separated communities. Wounds need healed.

Because of "Protestants and the papacy," I was turned down for the chair at the prominent evangelical school. In 2006 I noticed that a position became available at Marquette University, another Jesuit institution, about 100 miles north of Skokie in Milwaukee, Wisconsin. My son was in his sophomore year of high school and my wife had gone back to school to complete her degree so she could be the nurse manager of the oncology unit at the local hospital. I was not looking to move from Skokie, but I had such a good experience at St. Joseph's that I thought maybe I was a better fit for the Jesuits than my own Methodists. I applied and was offered the position in 2007. Instead of moving, I bought a pass on the Hiawatha Amtrak line that runs between Chicago and Milwaukee and exchanged the bicycle commute for the train for the next four years. I would take the early morning train to Milwaukee four days a week, stop off at the rec center, ride an indoor bicycle (which I despise) for thirty minutes, and catch the 5:45 evening train, arriving back to Skokie at 7 PM. Marquette turned out to be a much better fit; I did not mind the commute. The quiet car, the last car on the train, became my library, making possible two-and-one-half uninterrupted hours to research and write four days a week for four years. My cycling took a hit, but my research and publications benefited. During summer break, I would occasionally bicycle the ninety miles from my house in Skokie to my office in Milwaukee in the morning, take the train back in the evening, return the next day by train, and ride my bike back to Skokie.

Since writing "Protestants and the papacy" in 2005, I have repeatedly been asked, "Why are you not Catholic?" A decade later, after having worked at Marquette for eight years and deciding not to become Catholic, I thought it was time to answer that question directly, which I did in another editorial in the *Christian Century*.[7] During that decade, I regularly attended Catholic Mass, although I never received. I offered several reasons for not becoming Catholic, despite my increasing affection for, and influence by, the Catholic tradition. One significant reason was because I did not know how to become Roman Catholic without a sense of betraying the people who taught me to love God, to pray, to worship, to desire the Eucharist, take delight in Scripture, and so on. How can I leave the people I love? I remember my Methodist pastor, Lloyd Willert, who tended to me when I had my back surgery at the age of nineteen and lost the ability to run. He visited and prayed with me. After his death, when I went to seminary, his wife gave me books from his library. Then there was brother Cleveland Tennyson, a self-educated Afro-Caribbean local Methodist preacher that I worked with in Honduras for one year. His sermons brought me into the presence of God such that you had to take off your shoes when he preached because you were standing on holy ground. Geraldine Ingram was the first Methodist preacher I worked with in an official capacity. Her celebration of the Eucharist was beautiful and inspiring. It made me see the incarnation in a new light. Then there are numerous friends and family who have asked me not to convert. How could I walk away from Marvin, Shirley, Pattie, Lois, and Ricka, who gathered with me on Wednesday nights to be accountable in our discipleship, attend to Sunday's lectionary Gospel lesson, and celebrate the Lord's Supper together? It is not what I am against that keeps me Methodist; it is what I am for.

I had, largely out of frustration with Protestant sentimentality, decided to become Catholic on two occasions prior to joining the faculty at Marquette and initiated the process. On both occasions I had to wait because I had also been asked to lead a retreat, preach or preside at a Methodist Church, teach Sunday School class, lecture to a Methodist audience, or otherwise work in a local congregation. In Graham Greene's novel *The Power and the Glory*, a less-than-admirable whiskey-loving priest becomes holy, and possibly a saint, even though he had begun to question most of the Church's teachings, simply because he had too much going on to leave Mexico after a revolution that ousted the Catholic Church. I sometimes think I'm like a whiskey-loving Methodist preacher, without of course any claim to sainthood. I just never get around to leaving; I always have something to do for the Methodists that prevents it.

The 2005 editorial cost me a job at a Protestant evangelical institution. My Catholic friend and collaborator Michael Budde, a political philosopher, told me at the time that I should think of it as being fired before I got hired, a gracious preemptive strike.[8] He was correct. I did not belong there and given what happened with evangelical Christianity in the decades since, I was spared being miserable. I don't always know how to make sense of it, but I prefer working in a Catholic context or, as I do now, a more secular one that allows me to teach theology without demanding confessions of faith that require acts of mental contortions to sign them.

Of course, many Protestant conversions to Catholicism are themselves *protestant* conversions. On one occasion when I was tempted to convert to Catholicism, I did so because I was so angry at the silliness occurring among the Methodists, such as puppet and clown Eucharists, that I could not take it. My good friend Brent Laytham, another Methodist pastor and dean of the Ecumenical Institute in Baltimore, understood, but asked me to wait one year to make sure that I was not converting because of what I was protesting against. Would such a conversion not be one more act of protest? It was good Ignatian counsel coming from a Methodist. I waited the year, and then went through spiritual direction with a Jesuit to discern if I should convert. He did not think I was ready. I agreed.

How thorough is a Protestant conversion to Catholicism if the convert harbors a reactive protest against Protestantism? I am not a Methodist because I am in protest against Catholicism. I do think the church stands in need of constant reform, but need for reform should not be understood as a Protestant versus Catholic position. Catholics have often been better at reform than Protestants, as no less a Protestant than Karl Barth acknowledged after Vatican II. Yet I think that the Catholic Church needs reform. I find the absence of women in leadership deeply problematic. I sometimes wish Catholic bishops would at least run some of their statements past their mothers or sisters before releasing them to the public. I unequivocally support women's ordination. I don't have any grand theory of it; I have simply seen it bear spiritual fruit. I grew up with women preachers whose sermons bore the fruit of the Holy Spirit. They bring a unique perspective to the church that I think the church lacks if it denies them the exercise of their gifts. I think it matters that women were the first proclaimers of the resurrection and that the first person to make God present in his materiality was Jesus' mother.

I am concerned about abuses of authority and power that occur and have occurred in Roman Catholicism. Who could possibly deny this? I am concerned about habits of power that prompt Roman Catholic leadership toward secrecy or toward using the instruments of government to impose a way of life that Catholic laity themselves refuse to adopt. Let me give an example of the latter. I support the "Affordable Care Act" and would take it further. Supporting health care for everyone seems to me to be one way of fulfilling a command Jesus gave to us to love our neighbor. Catholic institutions should be allowed to opt out of any mandatory requirements for abortion or contraception. However, that Catholic (and some Protestant) leadership made this a question of persecution is dishonest. Many Catholic institutions were already providing contraceptive options for their employees prior to the Affordable Care Act.

Rather than taking on the federal government and claiming a loss of religious freedom, Catholic leadership, bishops, theologians, and laity would have been more truthful if they said to the Catholic people, "Artificial contraception is a question of mortal sin. We refuse to admit to the Eucharist, or receive money, from every Catholic person who violates this teaching. We will take the name 'Catholic' away from every institution already involved in this practice." Mind you, I don't think Catholic leaders should do this; it would be imprudent. I like the fact that Catholicism has an earthy paganism to it that can incorporate all kinds of messiness into its life. But if Catholic leadership is going to howl about persecution because they are asked to do something by the federal government that the Catholic people are already doing, then their witness rings hollow. I worry about a reactionary Catholicism that finds persecution when its moral teachings are not honored or implemented by governmental power but looks the other way when the majority of Catholic laity refuse them.

I confess I don't affirm Catholic teaching on contraception. When I was a Methodist pastor in Honduras in a village with many Catholics and Methodists, a priest from Miami would fly in every other month, drive to the Catholic Church in his Mercedes, unlock the church, hold Mass, lock the building, and drive off. I remember a poor Catholic woman in her early thirties who gave birth to her tenth child on a dirt path on her way to the clinic. She was faithful to the church, which I respect, but there was no one there to attend to her, to help her with her poverty or teach her NFP.

I also recall a conversation I once had with a young priest over dinner. He was going on and on about how everything in Western society declined once contraception was permitted. I was thinking to myself, contraception rather than slavery, genocide, Jim Crow, total warfare, white supremacy, patriarchy? I finally confessed to him that I had been married for more than two decades, did not follow Catholic teaching, and did not think my marriage embodied any of the consequences he thought inevitable from failing to do so. He turned to me and said, "Your marriage lacks the fullness it could otherwise have." I admit I was offended and wondered how a young priest could make such a snap judgment without knowing me, my wife, or our biological realities. I agree with Paul Ramsey, a Protestant ethicist, that marriage should be open to children over the lifetime of the marriage; it is part of the vocation to Christian marriage. I teach this when I do marital counseling. However, I do not think every act of sexual intercourse has to be open to it. Here I don't think I differ that far from Catholic teaching. NFP is itself a contraceptive practice that requires certain artificial instruments for its employment (thermometers, calendars, etc.). It is, however, unclear to me that it bears a different intentionality from certain other forms of "artificial" contraception. So if this teaching is necessary for someone to be Catholic, I am not Catholic.

Reformation is a temporal measure. Perhaps the time for reunion will come in my lifetime, perhaps not. In the meantime, those individuals who return prior to that day must not merely deepen the divide and therefore bear witness against that future reunion. How Catholics receive Protestant converts (and vice versa) will assist in this. If they are bounty in a culture war, then they are not faithfully received. One of my close friends, my son's godmother, left the Methodists and became Catholic. I am pleased she found a home and rejoice with her, just as I am pleased my daughter did as well. Another cradle Catholic friend wrote to her and said, "Welcome home. Sorry we left the house in such a mess." On the day we are reconciled, I hope the Catholic Church will welcome us with this kind of humility.

Marquette and the Jesuits were a good fit for me. While I was there, they had a strong ecumenical focus in their graduate theology program. It made for exciting and fruitful conversations. I had enjoyable colleagues, excellent students, and discovered a deep sense of happiness. However, the spatial distance between Skokie where I was living and Marquette where I was teaching was difficult. The trains ran every two to three hours. If an emergency arose, I had no way to get home except to wait for the next available train. An emergency did arise, one that led to a day more difficult than October 11, 2020.

FAMILIAL FRACTURES

The day before Ash Wednesday 2010 my son attempted to take his life during his second college semester. I was giving my final lecture on the Tuesday before Ash Wednesday and the beginning of Lent, when my phone buzzed repeatedly in my pocket. The moment class finished I checked my messages only to hear the following from my son's college roommate: "Jonathan left a suicide note and we cannot find him. We called security." Panic ensued. I flew back to my office, frantically calling Ricka and anyone who might have information. I wanted to get home as quickly as possible, but the next train was not due for two hours. I called taxis, buses, but nothing could get me home quicker than waiting for the train. I waited in my unknowing, fearful, out of control. Jonathan's roommate called again and told me that security found him and rushed him to the ER. After repeated calls to the hospital and what seemed an eternity of not knowing, we learned that Jonathan arrived in time and was in stable condition. My train to Skokie finally arrived. Ricka and I hopped in our car and drove through the night from Chicago to Cincinnati, passing into the season of Lent.

Sufficient time has passed for me to tell this story. My son is in a healthy place these days and I have his permission as well as his and my family's encouragement to tell it. We were surprised by our son's suicide attempt. He appeared happy and successful, active in church and youth group, a member of theater, the symphony, the choir, an all-conference swimmer surrounded by friends and family. We did not see it coming. Nor was his attempt one of those half-hearted attempts confused adolescents sometimes make. Had security not found him in the nick of time, he would have died. I've known parents who were not as fortunate as we were; security did not arrive in time and I mourn their loss. It is difficult to tell them our story because our story does not have the tragic ending that theirs does.

When we retrieved Jonathan from the hospital on Ash Wednesday, we saw a young man we hardly recognized, broken, disheveled, irrational, embarrassed, defiant. We drove him home and institutionalized him close to us so we could visit daily. We had no idea what to expect when we brought him home. After six months of close supervision, he seemed healthy enough to return to the university. Shortly after that our son called to tell us that he was dating someone—a man. His coming out did not take us completely by surprise. He had dated women in high school and college; he was dating a woman when he attempted suicide, so we were caught somewhat off guard, but women never really turned his head. I confess that there was some grief when he came out to us, but not because he was gay. We had too many gay friends, colleagues, and family members to find homosexuality itself a source of grief. The grief was found in my own imagining what his future life would be, something I had to learn to abandon because it had more to do with me than him. But even more than grief, there was relief. His previous struggles made sense and it became clearer how we could be supportive.

I had given much thought to homosexuality prior to my son's coming out, having written two essays on it. The issue was familiar since my days at Taylor University when my first gay friend came out to me in 1981. He and I prayed together for several semesters that God would remove his same-sex attraction. He was earnest and sincere. Our prayers were never answered. It did not occur to me back then that his attraction was as natural to him as opposite-sex attraction was to me. Of course, a sexual orientation is not in itself a normative, moral position, and not all desires are in themselves "natural." There are "unnatural" desires. By "natural" here I mean those creaturely dispositions that can be directed to good ends. Both of us would have to learn how to act morally on our orientation. He and I never made it to that discussion.

I had been aware of the moral debate over homosexuality before meeting my friend at Taylor. Anita Bryant came to my small Midwestern town when I was in high school, sponsored by several local churches. She was a leading voice back in the 1970s in spreading a message that the "gay agenda" would destroy Western civilization. I attended the rally as an evangelical Christian and even then was disturbed at the vitriol directed toward gay persons. It did not seem to fit with what I read in Scripture about loving one's neighbor. I heard friends, supposedly evangelical Christians, profess that they would "beat those gays up" if they came into our town, with little awareness that they were already there or that violence exercised toward gays invited God's displeasure rather than pleasure.

Much has changed since then, and I think undoubtedly for the better. Gay, lesbian, transgender, and intersex persons need no longer hide in the shadows. They are not forced into lifeless heterosexual marriages. Unfortunately, change has not gone far enough and many LGTBQI people still face violent abuse. Yet many no longer live in the shadows and because of their courage, they and others are less in danger of losing jobs, facing criminal charges, or being harassed and beaten by people who consider themselves to be executing divine judgment. Anyone who does not acknowledge the benefits of civil protections for LGBTQI persons not only lacks a moral compass but also poses an existential threat to my family and many others'. Civil rights extended to persons who are gay, lesbian, transgender, or intersex is a remarkable achievement, something I celebrate with joy, and something most churches now affirm. I think of this progress similar to how I think about civil rights extended to African Americans.

My son's emotional and mental health vastly improved when he came out. I knew the statistics that gay and lesbian adolescents were more likely to commit suicide than others. Now I *knew* it in a way that was less theoretical. My son's coming out also challenged me to learn from his life and think again as a moral theologian about homosexuality. Here is what I think I have learned. First, same-sex attraction is natural to some people. This first lesson should be recognized as a scientific advance similar to the fact that the earth is round and not the center of the universe, and humans evolved from previous life forms. Despite popular narratives around these issues, the church did not universally deny them but found ways to read Scripture well without abandoning reason, even when these facts appeared to conflict with straightforward interpretations of Genesis 1. Such a flat-footed reading of Scripture had been rejected by theologians as early as the second century, when careful exegetes recognized that the sun and the moon, necessary for a day, were created on the fourth day. Whatever "day" signified in Genesis 1, it could not mean the same as what day means for us. Scripture was not abandoned but read with richer allegorical and moral meanings.

We too must not abandon Scripture. It also appears to reject homosexuality. As is well known, and Scripture itself conveys, the story of Sodom and Gomorrah in Genesis 19 is not about homosexuality but inhospitality (Ezekiel 16:49–50). The crucial passage is Leviticus 18:22: "You shall not lie with a man as with a woman. It is an abomination." This passage occurs in the context of Moses reminding Israel that they are not to be like the other nations. They are not to be like the Egyptians from whom they have been redeemed nor like those in Canaan to whom God is bringing them (Leviticus 18:4). They are to be holy as God is holy. How they exercise their sexuality will be a sign of that holiness. The mission, of course, is not to be like the nations for the sake of the nations (Genesis 12:1–3). Sexual activity is not singled out as an issue apart from that mission. Leviticus 18:22, then, makes sense in terms of this mission. If a passage is taken out of the context of the mission to holiness and turned into a self-standing moral prohibition, then it will lose its intelligibility. God created male and female for a purpose. Our creation as male and female is a creaturely good that serves the command "be fruitful and multiply" (Genesis 1:27). Any rejection of maleness and femaleness is a rejection of fulfilling Scripture's first command. New Testament rejection of homosexuality in Romans 1, 1 Corinthians 6:9–10, and 1 Timothy 1:10 most likely assumes the prohibition in Leviticus 18:22, the mission in Genesis 12, and the purpose for male and female in Genesis 1.[9]

Does this mean that all male and female creatures are required to fulfill the command to procreate? Is this the sole reason for our sex and gender? If so, then Jesus did not fulfill the law. Celibacy shows that the command to be fruitful in Genesis 1 is not intrinsic to being male and female. Nor do we consider infertility to be divine judgment against sexually active heterosexual couples; we do not consider infertile heterosexual marriages invalid. Nor do we consider marriage among people past childbearing ages improper. Nor do we consider that all sex in marriage is morally permissible only when it issues in offspring. All churches recognize that there are goods of marriage beyond the good of procreation. What purpose does the prohibition against homosexuality serve? Is it a violation of creaturely goods present in created order?

The question may seem odd; a prohibition is a prohibition. If Scripture condemns something who are we to ask about what purpose it serves? But this is a necessary question because no one takes every prohibition in Scripture as a bare prohibition without asking what purpose the law, principle, or rule serves. Jesus himself set the context of the law in its fulfillment, not in its bare observance. Take the following examples. Many more could be raised.

> Jesus said, "But I say to you that everyone who divorces his wife, except on the grounds of unchastity, makes her an adulteress, and whoever marries a divorce woman commits adultery." (Matthew 5:32)

> Jesus said, "Lend, expecting nothing in return." (Luke 6:36)

In each of these cases, the bare observance of the law without concern for the purpose that it serves could have the effect of keeping the law but violating its purpose. Jesus said nothing about homosexuality, but he explicitly condemned divorce and remarriage. Most Protestant churches regularly remarry divorced people with little concern for the letter of the law. How did that come about? It could be a failure of biblical obedience, and perhaps on some occasions it is. My grandfather's treatment of my grandmother remains for me a sign of moral failure. But divorce is also permitted because we know of situations in which divorce and remarriage is more merciful than requiring people to stay together. When one person is being abused by another physically or emotionally such that the purposes of fidelity and friendship in marriage are so marred that they are no longer recognized, divorce and the possibility of remarriage fulfills the purpose of marriage better than forcing persons to stay in miserable conditions.

Who is kept up at night worrying that their savings and investments are making money in direct violation of Jesus' teaching to lend without interest? This may very well be a result of greed, but it may also be due to the fact that we recognize investments can generate nonexploitative profits that can be socially shared, such as sovereign wealth funds that can contribute to human flourishing. The bare observance of a prohibition because it is a prohibition is an act of fideism that makes it impossible to sustain ordinary moral living. It cannot take place with the mere observance of biblical law and the regular enforcement of every violation. It never has and it never will. This by no means entails that every precept, rule, or law should regularly be violated. It requires recognizing that laws are not an end in themselves but require an acknowledgment of their purposes for their intelligibility. As Thomas Aquinas put it, law directs human acts to virtuous ends. Lose those ends and the law becomes arbitrary. It serves no purpose.

Is homosexuality a violation of creaturely goods in the created order? Should we treat Leviticus 18:22 like we treat the prohibition against incest in Leviticus 18:9 or offering your children as sacrifices in Leviticus 18:21? Both practices violate creaturely goods, causing serious harm. Their prohibitions should be observed. Or should we treat it like we treat Matthew 5:32 and Luke 6:36? The answer to this question will depend upon the answer as to what purpose the prohibition against homosexuality serves. An answer to that question returns us to Genesis 1. What God gave to Israel that neither the Egyptians nor the Canaanites had was a creation story in which being created as male and female was a creaturely good. What some fear about homosexuality is that if it is affirmed, we will lose this creaturely good. The body becomes an inert thing with no moral significance until we exercise our will upon it. I find this to be a legitimate, but overwrought, concern in late modern capitalist society. Some fear a kind of dystopian future in which no child will be attributed a gender at birth, but parents will be required to wait until the child is of age to decide for her or himself what his or her gender will be. Then, after that decision, gender assignment will take place. What I learned most from my son's journey over the past ten years is that the latter fear is misplaced, and homosexuality raises little concerns about the former. Oh, there will always be some foolish person somewhere who will make outrageous claims like the current anti-natalists who judge every birth as an act of injustice. But the fear that we will lose the creaturely goods of maleness-femaleness because we allow same-sex marriage or acknowledge transgender and nonbinary persons is a fear that creaturely goods are neither creaturely nor goods. In other words, creaturely goods are what they are because God has made them, reflecting God's own goodness. Their goodness will endure. They do not depend upon our will to be sustained. If they do, if the only way to maintain the goodness of male-female relations is to willfully legislate against LGBTI people, then we tacitly deny the creaturely goods of being male and female. They are only goods through the power of our will and voluntary legislation.

That my son's same-sex orientation is as natural to him as my opposite-sex orientation is to me in no way violates that we are both male because what it means to be male is not simply that a person is willing to fulfill the command in Genesis 1. In fact, my grandfather "fulfilled" that command five times with my grandmother and then abandoned her and his children to poverty and the generosity of others for their sustenance. Surely sex serves other purpose than mere procreation. Celibacy is possible. Non-procreative elderly marriages are possible. Non-procreative infertile marriages are possible. Non-procreative heterosexual marriages for the sake of mission or under some dire consequences should be possible. Non-procreative same-sex marriages are possible ways to fulfill the mission laid out in Genesis 12. Such marriages fulfill the purposes of fidelity, friendship, and openness to life signifying the union between Christ and his church, drawing natural same-sex orientations into a grace-filled, sanctifying relationship.

The term *marriage* needs some clarity. There is, on the one hand, secular or civic marriage, which is a legal contract people enter into on the basis of rights to negotiate property. In the US, it is now open to all on an equal basis, as it should be. There is, on the other hand, the Christian vocation to marriage. As a vocation it is a calling to a specific form of life. It is the task of the local ecclesial community to determine if any two persons are called to marriage. Included in the vocation for heterosexual couples is an openness to children through biological reproduction insofar as that is possible. Bearing and raising children is a moral endeavor grounded in creaturely goods. We all came into existence through the creation of male and female. To deny this is to deny the conditions for our own existence. There are also other forms of the marriage vocation; the marriage of the elderly for the sake of companionship and that of those who have a natural same-sex orientation for similar reasons. Some same-sex oriented persons, like other-sex oriented persons, might be called to celibacy, but no one should be forced to be celibate because of their vocation or sexual orientation. When that occurs, it is an invitation to deception.

Gay, lesbian, and transgender persons and communities need the church as much as straight persons and communities do. The church also needs gay, lesbian, and transgender persons to fulfill its mission well. They pose no greater challenge to creaturely goodness than do straight persons. That some people are born both male and female, a biological fact that makes possible a nonbinary account of gender, need not challenge the creaturely goodness of male and female either, although their presence among us does challenge what it means to be *either* male *or* female. If gay, lesbian, transgender, or intersex persons were incapable of recognizing sexual difference they would be unrecognizable as gay, lesbian, transgender, and intersex persons. Fear not. We are not headed into a dystopian future. We are attempting to make space for persons made in the image of God who have been silenced and marginalized for centuries, and whose natural desires, orientations, and biological realities need sanctifying grace that will require something other than individual moral heroism because the only option the church gives them is to "voluntarily" choose enforced celibacy. "Force" and "voluntary" contradict each other.

Readers may say that I have only come to these arguments and conclusion because of the trauma of my son's attempted suicide. My answer is yes, of course. Ordinary life can be an excellent moral teacher; that basic insight is one reason why I wrote this book. This should be no more controversial than the fact that the complete failure of my heart caused me to rethink questions of life and death in a new way. The difficulty of being same-sex oriented almost destroyed my son's life, as it has for many. I enter every Lent with gratitude that unlike many my son was restored to me. Yes, that restoration made me rethink things, but it made me *rethink* things. My son is a musician. Reflecting on his own dark night of the soul, he wrote a song, "Excuse me Lord." Let me conclude these reflections with the lyrics he wrote.

> Excuse me lord,
> but would you mind,
> If I prayed to you,
> I know it's been some time
> but I've lost my way,
> when I found myself,
> refused help but now I realize.
> I need someone,
> someone like you,
> someone who knows,
> what we do when we've got something,
> we've misplaced,
> we just can't say,
> It's on the heart,
> it's on the brain,
> It's something I just can't explain.
> It's like when you've been broken down,
> It's like when you've been beat around, listen to the sound,
> It can't be found maybe,
> It's way too loud maybe,
> I scream and shout but it don't come out and now I'm drowning
> in it.
> They tell me:
> The way you live is not allowed,
> your presence just might change a crowd,
> You're just a sinner baby,
> It's unforgiven baby,
> There's something wrong and you don't belong,
> but I'm still praying lately!
> I can't see how this will play out,
> but the lights have dimmed and I'm overwhelmed

thinking I'm the one that it's all about
and I'm scared with how it will all turn out,
but the show goes on with you or without
and they still believe even with a doubt,
that the ones they love just might be pushed out,
just because you are something that stands out.
I can't see how this will play out,
but the lights have dimmed and I'm overwhelmed
thinking I'm the one that it's all about
and I'm scared with how it will all turn out,
but the show goes on with you or without
and they still believe even with a doubt,
that the ones they love just might be pushed out,
just because you are something that stands out.

BROKEN BONES AND BROKEN BIKES

One year after my son's ordeal, Ricka and I moved to Wisconsin. Once again, we looked for a home along a good cycling commute and I took up my old practice. The quickest route was four miles in traffic; the safest was seven miles along the Hank Aaron State Trail that included side trails that I could ride for extra mileage without the need to be attentive to automobile traffic. I would also add laps on the one-mile circuit around Miller Park, the baseball stadium where the Brewers play. It barely had traffic that time of day. I would ride longer than the commute to keep my mileage to a thirty-mile daily average. Working in a pleasant environment with colleagues who trusted and respected me and recovering my daily bicycle ride brought happiness. Life was good and not even the events that occurred in late October 2011 changed that, although they placed a barricade to it.

Bicycle commuting requires factoring in sufficient time for the occasional flat tire, the necessary shower and clothing change, and other potential problems that arise. I estimated an extra twenty minutes for "just in case" situations. Three decades of commuting had proven that was sufficient time. On one gray, crisp October morning I rode into Marquette. As far away from my office as I would be that day, I heard that sound no cyclist wants to hear: pssssss. Sure enough, the rear tire was losing air rapidly. I stopped, fixed it, and took off. I looked at the time and realized I still had enough to make it to class. One mile down the road the annoying sound found its way into my ears yet again: psssss, a second flat, this time on the front tire. Two flats on different tires are unusual and now I was more than annoyed. I would barely have time to make it to class. Having repaired the second flat, I took off, hammering as fast as I could to get to Marquette in time for a shower and change of clothes before class began. It was going to be tight.

A slight downhill into a four-way stop stood between me and the bike trail that led to the last few miles of the commute. At that time of day, cars were seldom at the intersection. I decided to blow through the four-way stop before the trailhead, looking left and right to make sure no cars were doing the same. All was clear as I entered and exited the intersection. I looked up at the last instance to see that I was going to miss the entrance to the trail. A large curb marked off with yellow paint sat on both sides of the entrance to the trail. In my haste, I had mistaken the yellow for the entrance. It was too late to stop. I hit the curb at well over twenty mph. The impact broke my carbon fiber bike in half, which may have been a good thing because rather than going straight into the concrete I flew into it like a forward slide in baseball, except this was much faster and into concrete. I laid there dazed, probably in shock.

Three cars passed in the minutes after the crash. One did not stop. The second did and asked if I was okay as I lay on the ground. I told the driver that I thought I was, and he drove off. Adrenaline was flowing through my body; it tends to ward off the pain momentarily. I stood up, looked at my busted bicycle, and tried to pick it up. Shooting pain ran through my mangled and bloody hands. I could not wrap my hands around the bike. A third driver, named Ahmed, stopped and asked how I was. I told him that I didn't know. Shock and pain clouded my thinking, and he knew I needed help. He asked where I was headed, and I told him Marquette. He put my busted bicycle in the trunk of his car, assisted me into the passenger side, and asked if that is where I wanted to go. I said, "Yes." He thought I should call someone and that seemed to make sense, so I called Ricka. As I was talking to her, he mentioned that there was blood coming from my ear. Come to find out, it was superficial, but I had broken bones in both my hands and one broken rib. Reason prevailed and we agreed it made no sense to go to Marquette. I needed to get to the hospital. Ahmed asked where I lived and graciously drove me home, setting my bicycle in a crumpled mess in the driveway.

Wanting to do some kind gesture in response to his, I asked if I could pay him for the ride. He guffawed and said of course not. I went into the house, took a shower, and waited for Ricka to arrive and drive me to the hospital.

I spent the next six weeks with casts on both my hands, unable to type, work around the house, or assist myself in daily bodily functions. Once again, my misfortune involved Ricka. The bulk of the housework fell to her. We had invited my family to Thanksgiving that year and I was unable to do much of anything. Several months after this, Ricka accidentally left the gas cap off our old Buick twice, running over it both times. The second time I remarked to her, "You know those gas caps are not cheap." She replied, "Yes, and how much was that carbon fiber bicycle?" Touché.

My first catastrophic crash was due to an irresponsible cyclist, the second to a dog, and a third to my own stupidity. Each took some time to recover. I have rehabbed from broken collar bones, ribs, shoulder surgery, and several back surgeries. This third crash involved some very small bones in my hands, yet nothing was as painful as the rehab to restore the use of my hands. After six weeks, the casts were removed, and I had my first visit with the physical therapist. She took my fingers and bent them back until tears streamed down my face. I take some pride in my ability to withstand pain, but this was too much. She noted my embarrassment and reassuringly said, "Don't worry. I've had Navy Seals who cried from this therapy." It was only the beginning. I was required to squeeze a ball five times a day and hold my fingers back for a certain period of time. Physical therapists are amazing healers. I have learned to listen to them and follow their directions to the letter even though they appear as something straight out of the Inquisition; they know how to cause pain. It is an inevitable part of healing.

One of the downsides of recovering from broken bones is time off the bike. With broken a collarbone, I could ride my bicycle indoors within one week. Broken hands made this impossible. I could not put any weight on my hands, not even to lay them on the handlebars. Plus, having broken my bike in half, I no longer had a bicycle to ride. My carbon fiber Trek 5200 lay in the garage in pieces. I only had one bike. We had just moved and purchased a new house and did not have the money to buy another one. Less than one year after moving to Wisconsin, I found myself in Marquette's rec room once again riding gingerly on a standing indoor bicycle until I recovered sufficiently to ride outdoors. In the meantime, I considered how I could acquire another bicycle.

I had heard that carbon fiber bikes can be repaired and sent pictures of my busted bicycle to a carbon repairman. Nope, he said, not when it is broken like this. In fact, he said, I should consider myself fortunate to have lived through such an accident and the best I could do with that bike is mount it as wall art as a warning what not to do on a bicycle. I got the point. I purchased a heavier, steel Surly frame and had the component parts of the busted Trek transferred to it so that I would have a commuting bike. I use that bike for commuting to this day; its component parts are a constant reminder not to do stupid things on a bicycle. A decent top-end bicycle cost around $4,000 and we did not have the money. Unbeknownst to me, Ricka contacted her nephew who raced bicycles with some success and was the member of a team. She asked him if he knew of anyone with a good used bicycle my size that would be willing to sell. He did and she purchased a 2011 Cannondale Supersix as a surprise for me. I loved that bike; it was by far the best bike I had possessed up to that time. I managed to crash it as well.

The next two catastrophic crashes were not due to my own stupidity but due to poor infrastructure in Milwaukee and Dallas. Wisconsin and Texas do not share much in common. Our annual transition from one to the other is something of a culture shock, but one thing they do share is poor road conditions. February 4th, 2014 in Wisconsin was a very cold Tuesday. The Spokesmen hold a regular ride at 5:45 every Tuesday, Thursday, and Friday morning, year-round. In the winter, we ride bikes with studded snow tires and keep the pace slow. Only three of us showed up that morning. I was on my Surly. It was freezing, something like five degrees. Two really strong riders showed up, Fast Freddy and Kayzar. As part of their camaraderie, the Spokesmen tended to give everyone a nickname or call them something other than their forename. I became known as Doc Long. Fast Freddy's nickname is obvious. We were doing a brief fifteen-mile ride from Wauwatosa to the Harley Davidson museum and back. Even at the slower winter pace, I worked hard to keep up with them. The difficult part of the ride was behind us. We had a downhill to a coffee shop for warmth and coffee. It was still dark. I was riding behind Fast Freddy and to the right of Kayzar when suddenly I found myself slammed into the sidewalk on the side of the road. Because of the darkness, I had not seen a large gap that had opened up in the road. My wheel had fallen into it, throwing me off the bike. I immediately knew it was my collarbone. Fast Freddy and Kayzar helped me into the nearby McDonald's and waited with me in the warmth until Ricka showed up and took me yet again to the hospital. There is an unstated rule among the Spokesmen that you don't leave anyone behind, especially on frigid Wisconsin days. I don't know if Frederick and Jason were late to work that day, but they waited with me despite my protestations. I was grateful for their assistance.

Several crashes occurred from my last broken bone in 2014 to my cardiac incident in 2020. As previously mentioned, on Saturday, March 3, 2018, I was riding in the peloton on the South Loop in Dallas. We turned onto McKenzie Road, a notoriously bad road with broken pavement and huge potholes. When riding in a peloton, the rider in front is responsible to point out dangers such as road debris, potholes, and gaps in the road. Sometimes roads are so bad that no one wants to let go of their handlebars to indicate dangerous conditions. McKenzie is like that. It has a downhill followed by a steady climb. We were on the downhill anticipating the climb. I was stuck to the wheel in front of me when he slightly moved, and I found my wheel dipping into a gap in the road. My hands came off the handlebars, my chest hit them, and I fell to the pavement, sliding across its rough surface. Given how bad the road conditions are on McKenzie, I cannot blame the rider in front of me. When roads are in such disrepair, the peloton becomes a Hobbesian war of all against all; no one dare remove a hand from the handlebars.

What is remarkable is that I had the perfect crash at a relatively high speed in the midst of a peloton and I was the only one to go down. I slid in the direction of my bike and the rider behind managed to react in time to avoid going down. Had he gone down, or had I been thrown into bikes on my left or right, it could have caused a massive pileup. No one wants to be responsible for that, even if it was beyond their control. I hit the ground with such force that my helmet cracked, but my much loved Supersix bicycle appeared to be okay. Massive road rash and contusions marked the right side of my body, but no bones were broken. After a crash, a bike should be checked out to make sure it is not dangerous to ride. Riding an unfit bike is a potential hazard not only to its rider but to other riders as well. I later rode my Supersix to the bike shop to have it inspected. The tube of the front fork that fits into the headset, something that cannot be seen without taking the head set apart, was damaged. I was told it was too dangerous to ride home.

The March 3 crash was fortunate in that no bones were broken. It was unfortunate because I was once again reduced to my Surly commuting bike. It was inconvenient because that evening my daughter Lindsey called and told us that she had gone into labor. Ricka indulged my cycling habit throughout our marriage but she was not going to miss the birth of our granddaughter. She hopped on the first available flight and landed in Chicago fearful that she would be late for the delivery. She announced to the other passengers that her daughter was in labor and they graciously allowed her to exit the plane first. She hurried to baggage claim and waited a few minutes for her luggage, but it did not come fast enough. Becky and Adam, who live in Milwaukee, just happened to be in Chicago. Adam told Ricka that he would pick her up at Midway Airport and drive her across Chicago to Evanston Hospital, where Harper was being born. Ricka left her bags at the airport, jumped into the car, and made it in time for delivery. Adam later drove back across the city to retrieve her luggage. Anyone who knows what it is like to drive across Chicago from Evanston to Midway Airport and back will know what an act of charity that was. I remained in Dallas to finish teaching my class and join her later in the week. I was scheduled to teach a Sunday school class at Highland Park United Methodist Church that Sunday on Christian ethics. After dropping Ricka off at the airport, covered with Tegaderm and more than a bit loopy, I went to church and made it through the class. Toward the end of the class, I received the message that our long-awaited Harper was here. I announced it to the class with joy. I had become a grandfather.

Visiting Harper in Adam and Lindsey's home in Chicago was nothing short of mystical. Grandchildren give you a second chance to see the world in all its newness and surprise. Smiling, then crawling, then walking, then talking, each new stage is a wonder to behold. Perhaps grandparenthood is so marvelous because there is no sleep deprivation. Perhaps it is the wisdom that comes with age, the ability to be present without striving for what comes next. Perhaps it is the more relaxed stage of life. Whatever it is, grandparenthood came with more patience simply to observe, to see, marvel, and reflect. I love to ride my bicycle along Lake Michigan from

Chicago through Evanston and further north. I know the roads well. When we visited Lindsey, Adam, Harper, and Emma, I took my bike and rode during Harper's nap. I prepared to ride a few minutes before she napped, putting on my kit and my shoes. She grew accustomed to this ritual early in her life. One day after putting on my kit, unprompted and before she could barely speak, Harper retrieved my helmet and placed it on my head.

Do we not tend to forget that someone labored on our behalf for us to be? Others' wounds become the source of our very existence. We forget the moral significance that at the beginning of life someone cleans us and changes our diapers, stays up at night and soothes us, feeds us and lays us down to rest. We want not to be reminded that the same will most likely happen at the end of our lives. Why is this? Perhaps we fear losing control, that tenuous hold we think we have over our actions and associate with being a moral agent. When we think of moral agency, we often think of individual subjects who can act voluntarily in the world based on their own decisions or even rules that they give themself. Yet ethical agency is seldom actually like that. Fractures, wounds, and scars can be reminders that life is a gift, that each of us, at some point, will need to be tended to by others, that we are incapable of closing the wounds or reconciling the divisions alone. It reminds us not to think of ethical agency primarily as acting from the strength of our independence, but to be open to receiving what life brings and making the most of it, to pay attention to the surprising gifts that come our way and accept them as graces, as works of the Holy Spirit.

In 1983, Bob was driving across the Midwest from Kansas to Indiana to be the best man at our wedding during a very hot July. Not only did his car not have air conditioning, but halfway across he was unable to turn off the heat. He drove with the windows down the rest of the way. He picked up a hitchhiker and drove with him for quite a time before stopping at a convenience store while the hitchhiker slept in the passenger seat. When Bob returned the hitchhiker was gone, nowhere to be seen. For a moment Bob thought that perhaps he had entertained an angel unaware. Then he noticed that one of the two ten-dollar bills he left sitting on the dashboard was missing. When he told me this story, he was grateful that his conversations with the hitchhiker had at least made an impression such that the hitchhiker only stole one ten-dollar bill and left the other one for him. Small graces well received become virtues of faith that give hope in the midst of this fractured world and enable acts of charity that make possible its wholeness.

4

The Middle

Where we always want to be

Contemplating death in the hospital bed in the ER on October 11 seemed unreal, as if I were living someone else's life. I also began to feel cheated. I was only sixty years old. Surely I had not yet come to the end; I was still in the middle. My mind raced to family and friends who had died about this age and I began to wonder if they knew what was befalling them as they entered into that dark night, or if like me they were perplexed, not sure exactly what was happening, even living in denial. Did they too feel something like this? Did they also have this inbuilt resistance? Not yet; not now; there is too much still to be done. Sophie and Emma were only five and three months old. I wanted to observe them rolling over, crawling, walking, talking. I wanted to hear them say "Pa Pa," the name Harper had given me and one that I'm sure they would think was normal, more my name than "Duane," or "Steve." My parents had named me Duane after my father Wayne. Mom thought I should be Wayne Jr., but Dad thought that was pretentious for someone from Buffalo. They settled for Duane. My older sister Diane, however, started calling me Steve and that stuck. Then I had children and bore the name "Dad." Now, late in life I was named yet again, "Pa Pa." I am also "Reverend" and "Doctor," but no title brings as much joy as "Pa Pa."

There were things I still wanted to do. Perhaps that is how it always is at the end—you long to hang on to being in the middle. I wanted to celebrate Thanksgiving and Christmas with our family. I had been working on a book, *Infusing Virtue: Learning and Teaching Ethics,* for nearly a decade that, like this one, always seemed to get postponed. Significant progress had been made that semester. I was reading a biography of John Rawls on the day my heart stopped doing the research for that book. (I don't blame Rawls or Rawlsians for my fate!) I had graduate students to assist, sermons to preach, classes to teach. Because of coronavirus I had not seen my parents for months but hoped to spend ample time with them next summer at their lake house, once the pandemic subsided. I did not know what the outcome of the Methodist Church's divisions would be. The US election was ongoing. I had not yet voted nor seen how the crazy political situation the US was living through would come to an end. So much was going on. I was in the middle of too many things, things I wanted to see to completion.

We always are, which means that there is never a good time to die. Don't get me wrong. I recognize that life can become so difficult death is welcome. My sister-in-law Dannet, the mother of the nephew who secured a bike for me, died in her late forties of breast cancer. As an oncology nurse, Ricka spent months assisting in her care. Dannet wanted to die at home and Ricka helped make that possible. A hospital bed was moved into her dining room and she passed into that dark night with family surrounding her, singing hymns. If there is such a thing as a good death, hers was. But it was only good because it was an end to significant suffering. How much better it would have been if she could have been healthy and lived to see her sons married, her grandchildren, receive yet another name in her lifetime like I did in mine. What a delightful grandmother she would have been. She too was in the middle of many things, as was Ricka's sister Kim when she died having just turned fifty.

It is the middle where we desire to live, and wrongly imagine we are living because we assume that the end is distant, still far off in the future. Beginnings and endings are only known from the perspective of the middle. We don't know what the ending will be until we get there, and when we do, we discover what the beginning was for. But here's the thing, we seldom, if ever, get there. The end is as much a surprise as is the beginning. There are endings along the way: births, graduations, weddings, projects completed, funerals, but each of these endings remains for the living a new beginning because we always seem to be in the middle. None of us knows the end, except the one who was raised and said, "Be not afraid." But the end is frightening; it means that there is no more middle, and joy is found in the middle. Surely this is why we are commanded to "be not afraid." If it wasn't fearful, there would be no reason for the command.

THE CALIFORNIA BICYCLE JOURNEY

When Bob and I set off on our bicycles on May 18, 1982 to get from Indiana to California, the point was not to move from the beginning to an end; a car, train, or plane could have sufficed for that. The point instead was to experience life along the way, to live in the middle. We took off late morning and headed toward Buffalo, stopping first at my Aunt Jean's home and then Grandma Thelma's. They outfitted us with food and water and wished us well. We set a goal to ride 100 to 130 miles each day so we could arrive in Lake Tahoe by June 12, allowing for only a few days off. Most cyclists who ride across the US go west to east with the prevailing winds. We did not have that luxury and suffered the consequences of headwinds most of the way. One day in Nevada toward the end of our journey, the winds were so strong, and we were so exhausted, that for a time we stopped and walked as if we were protesting the weather. Wind has a diabolical agency, laughing in your face, sucking up your energy and dispersing it chaotically across the landscape. "Damn wind!" I often cursed it. Several days we rode through rain, and a few days rain and wind. We were wise enough not to ride in storms unless absolutely necessary. The second day out we wanted to get to Eureka, Illinois, about 200 miles from our origination in Wabash. A sudden storm appeared toward the end of the day, forcing us to change plans and stay in El Paso, Illinois, fourteen miles short of the day's goal. Two days in and we were already behind schedule; every mile lost would need to be made up.

Tired, sore, and already wondering why we thought this would be enjoyable, we mounted our bikes the third day and pleasantly discovered that the elevation from Eureka to Peoria, Illinois drops 270 feet over twenty-one miles. With an unusual tailwind, we made good time. Bob remarked in his journal (most of my account of our journey comes from his journal, since neither of us trust our memories forty years later) how exhilarating it was to ride that distance at a very fast pace and also how frightening to do so with panniers. The most significant downhill we rode in Indiana was an overpass. We were not experienced downhill cyclists. With full packs, a bicycle begins to shake at high speeds. The downhill into Peoria, however, was nothing like what we were headed to over the Rocky Mountains and other mountain ranges between us and Lake Tahoe. We learned to descend on the road, often putting our knees on the cross bars to steady our bikes.

We came across several cyclists on our journey. The first was a couple we met on the other side of Peoria. They had been riding around the country for two years. They offered us some of their marijuana; we declined. They made money along the way by the woman stripping and they asked us if we would like to pay to watch her strip; we declined again. Bob and I were rather naïve evangelicals for whom such invitations were abnormal. In fact, we were propositioned on two occasions as we rode, and if one counts our brief visit to a bordello, it would be three. Each time we declined. Those experiences let us know that we were no longer at Taylor. The world was much broader, and in many ways more interesting, than the isolated evangelical bubble in Upland, Indiana. The stripping couple told us that they got along with everyone along their journey except religious people. Bob and I remained quiet on that count.

Peoria, Illinois contains a little over 100,000 inhabitants. It was the largest urban area we rode through until we reached Denver, nearly 1,000 miles away. We rode through farmland in Indiana and Illinois, rolling hills in Iowa, and back to farmland in Nebraska and Kansas. Riding past row after row of corn on flat roads was mind-numbing, the most psychologically demanding part of our journey. I got so tired and bored after a few days that one afternoon I complained to Bob, "I've had it with this. I'm stopping." I pulled off the side of the road, got off my bike, laid down between two corn rows, and slept. After days of monotony, our spirits were buoyed when we first glimpsed the Rocky Mountains.

We became so familiar with our bicycles that we thought it appropriate to give them names. Mine was knighted "Chariot" and Bob's "Fire." Both were solid Schwinn bicycles, but packed out with rear panniers, a front bag, loaded down with food and water on the rear rack, and being ridden 100-plus miles day after day takes it toll. Only a few days in, my rear wheel went out of true, wobbling so that the tire rubbed the brakes. Nothing ruins a ride like a wheel out of true; it needed to be fixed. A cycling mechanic is called a "wrench," and every bike club has someone who is an excellent wrench, fascinated with the mechanical aspects of the bicycle. A wrench often works as an engineer, seldom as a theologian or minister. I am no wrench; neither was Bob. I despise working on my bicycle and do the least maintenance possible. We brought tools to fix issues that we thought we could handle. I tried to true the wheel on the road without a truing stand and only made it worse. I opened the brakes as wide as possible so the wobbling wheel would not rub against them and rode to the next town in hopes of finding someone who could true a wheel. We were far from any urban areas or bike shops, but we found a lawn mower repair shop in Donnellson, Iowa and asked the repairman if he thought he could fix it. He did what he could and did it for free when we told him of our journey.

We received many gifts like this along the way. Most evenings we slept in rural churches. Assuming the parsonage was the house next to the church, we would knock on the door and ask the pastor if we could sleep in the church. We told him (it was usually a male pastor) who we were, what we were doing, and why. I was considering seminary along with medical school and hoped to become a Methodist pastor. I think we were only turned down once. Many times, the pastor would invite us to stay in the parsonage, offering dinner and breakfast. The hospitality we received encouraged us. Plus, we only had $600 for the two of us and had to make it last as best we could.

Bob's brother lived in Denver and we took our first day off there. The mountains had loomed before us for several days, taunting us. The distance between them and us seemed never to lessen, as if they were moving with us. Eventually we arrived in Denver and were excited about leaving the flatland to ride through the mountains. Eleven straight days of 100-plus miles of riding gave us the opportunity to ride into shape. The soreness was gone; the bikes were working well. We were ready. Sunday May 30, we woke early at 5:30 to ride across Denver into the Rockies. Sixty miles separates downtown Denver from Loveland Pass. At an elevation of 11,999 feet, it is one of the highest passes in Colorado, a 6,711-foot difference from Denver. It was demanding but glorious. The scenery was spectacular, causing us to forget the monotony of Kansas.

We arrived at Loveland Pass in the afternoon and then dropped 2,000 feet on an eight-mile downhill into Dillon, where we stayed the night. The descent into Peoria was nothing like this. We were moving between forty and fifty mph, staying up with traffic, even needing to slow down because the cars could not take the turns as fast as we could. The pastor in Dillon was uncomfortable letting us stay in the church, but he permitted us to sleep on the porch. Fortunately, it had a roof; we woke up to snow. The next day began with another glorious 1,000-foot descent, this time into Vail. We were told about a bicycle trail into Vail and rode it while watching mountain goats play. The sixty-eight miles from Vail to Glenwood Springs were the most nerve-wracking cycling I have ever done. At that time, only one road could get you there, Interstate 70. Bicycles were permitted on the shoulder for several miles, including through tunnels; we were sharing the road with fast cars, trucks, and plenty of semis. The tunnels were horrifying. We would wait until the fewest cars possible were coming and speed through them as fast as possible. Signs were regularly posted, letting drivers know that bicycles were permitted and that it was legal for us to be there, for which we were grateful, but motorists were as displeased to discover us as we were to be suddenly overtaken by them. It was not until 2016 that a bicycle path opened up for that stretch; cyclists now have a more relaxed, less white-knuckle ride.

The next day we continued our journey in the Rockies to Grand Junction, Colorado. We came across a homeless fellow who told us his life story. He was hitching across the US by train and truck, and had been at Grand Junction for some time, making a comfortable life for himself. He knew exactly when the local fast-food restaurant threw out their food. He would wait by the dumpster and take the food for himself. Natural hot springs flow through parts of western Colorado. They have been dammed up and turned into commodities by local resorts. People pay good money to stay at a natural hot springs resort. The hot springs also flow into the Colorado River. Our homeless friend had walled off one of the runoffs into the river and turned it into his own private hot springs. He invited us to join him. We gorged that evening on free fast food while soaking in a hot spring. It was one of our most memorable evenings.

Riding along the Colorado River into Utah was as beautiful as riding through the Rocky Mountains, but Utah was deceiving. We had to cross several mountain passes; they could be seen in the distance. We rode mile after mile through relatively flat land, yet here too the distance to the mountain pass seemed always to be the same. It would take forever to arrive at the start of the climb. Then we went up, over, and down only to see in the distance another mountain pass, seemingly identical to the one we just climbed. There were miles and miles without any town or stores, so we had to make sure to have sufficient food and water. We were getting closer to California, only five or six days of riding remained when our trip almost ended prematurely.

Delta, Utah is the largest city in Millard County; it has about 3,000 people. It is so desolate that it sells itself as "the gateway to Nevada's Great Basin National Park, one of the country's least visited national parks due to its remote location." We headed out into that remote location and were ten miles west of Delta early Friday evening as the sun began to set. We had no choice but to sleep outside in the Utah desert. We were looking for the safest place to sleep when I pushed my pedal and almost fell off my bike. My pedals spun aimlessly as I rolled to a stop. The rear hub on my wheel broke so that the cogs would not engage the hub. We had no means to fix this problem and here we were in an area that billed itself as a "remote location." It was Friday evening, and we were still approximately 500 miles from our destination. It was disheartening. We began to wonder if our adventure was finished. There was no place to buy another rear wheel and we could not afford it if there was. We agreed that I would hitchhike the ten miles back into Delta and Bob would spend the night in the desert. I noted the surroundings, walked to the road with just my wheel, and stuck out my thumb.

The first truck that came along stopped and I explained the situation to the driver. He drove me back to Delta. There were not many stores in town, and of the few that there were, none were open on Friday evening except for a bar. I walked into the bar, dressed in my sweaty cycling clothes and carrying my bicycle wheel. I must have been an odd sight. Needless to say, I was immediately noticed. I asked if there was anyone who fixed bikes in town, or where the closest bike shop was. The closest shop was in Provo, Utah, ninety miles away. People had now begun to take an interest in my situation and one guy spoke up, "I know a guy two miles out of town who used to ride bikes. You might ask him." "Worth a try," I thought. I got the address, went back to the road, and put out my thumb to hitch another ride. A guy stopped. I told him the address and he said that was his brother's house. Getting into a strange car with a man outside a bar on a Friday evening in a remote location did not seem like the smartest thing I have done, but everyone in the bar at least knew who I was and what I had been doing. "If I disappear," I thought, "at least people will know where I was headed." I got in his car and he drove me to his brother's house. His brother happened to be home and told us that he did have a spare wheel from a Schwinn bicycle that he had crashed. It was lying under his porch. Sure enough, it was a perfect match for my bike. The brother then kindly drove me back to the spot where Bob was.

Bob's journal entry for that day is worth quoting. First he wrote, "What a day. Here I am all by myself in the desert being attacked by a thousand mosquitos. I'm so miserable. Steve had to go back to Delta by hitchhiking—his back hub is broken—about 10–15 miles to see if there is any way possible he could get it fixed. It's about 8:30 PM now and I must admit I'm a little scared." A few hours after I returned, Bob wrote, "The Lord sure worked a miracle. Steve hitched a ride in; some people in town knew of a guy who had a good bike two miles out. Steve got picked up by the guy's brother. He had a good back wheel [and] drove Steve to where I was. It was a miracle. If Steve didn't find a wheel we would have had to quit right there." His journal entry is not exaggerated. Indeed, it is hard not to see the charity of providence at work. Only a few hours after what we thought might be the end of our journey, I was back in the desert with Bob, experiencing the same mosquito onslaught. Given what had transpired, the mosquitoes did not seem so bad. We tucked into our sleeping bags as best as possible and got as much sleep as we could, grateful our journey would continue.

The next day we entered Nevada. We were in the desert, but a tremendous headwind cooled the temperatures to about fifty degrees. This was the day, June 6, that the wind was so ferocious that we lodged our protest, conceded to the wind, and out of disgust just walked for a time; the ultimate violation of at least Velominati rules #5, "HTFU," and #6, "free your mind and your legs will follow." There was no freeing of the mind in that wind. We were getting close to California but riding through the desolate desert was difficult; one day it was cold, the next hot. Because it was desolate, we each carried an extra gallon of water tied to our rear racks, as well as the water in our water bottles. I didn't pay close attention, the knots from my rope loosened, and the plastic water jug fell to the ground. The water poured out. We were in the middle of nowhere with only the water in Bob's jug remaining. We knew we needed more and stopped at the first place we found. It was an odd place, a ranch-style house surrounded by a fence with barbed wire and surveillance cameras. It did not look like a family residence. We were uncertain what it was, and a bit concerned, but desperate we decided Bob would ring the bell and ask the proprietors for water. He rang and the gate automatically opened. He went in the fence, up to the door, and knocked. I saw the door open and Bob disappear inside. Within a very short time (and I can testify it was a very short time), Bob reappeared. He was quite animated and said to me, "Steve, do you know what that was?" "No." "It was a brothel. The women were lined up when I went in and the madam asked me what I would like. When I realized what was going on, I said to her, 'I'm just looking for some water.' The women laughed. She filled up the water jugs and sent me on my way." We did not know that prostitution was legal in Nevada, but we discovered it was that day, which made for an interesting discussion all the way into Eureka, Nevada. How fitting that the charity of providence meets you in the most surprising places.

By June 8 we were almost out of money. With only one or two more days of riding until our destination, we stopped at a Safeway in Fallon, Nevada to buy peanut butter and bread. It was cheap and full of protein and had become a staple along the way. When we could afford it, we would buy jelly as well, but we knew that was not an option with our dwindling resources. A jar of peanut butter and a bag of white bread would last until Tahoe. A young girl named Laura was shopping with her parents when she spotted us, recognizing that we were cyclists. She struck up a conversation and asked us if we would like to spend the night with her family. Convinced that a young girl did not have permission to invite two strangers into her home, we declined. She recognized our hesitation and told us that her parents were in the next aisle and that they always invited cyclists to stay with them. Her brother had been a cyclist and it was a way of returning a favor. She took us to her parents, who not only invited us to stay with them but also paid for our groceries. It was a lovely Mormon family. We stayed with them the next day and they told us their story. Their son, the cyclist, had struggled with mental illness. He had taken his life during a church service. Their story was heart-wrenching. They were incredibly kind to us. Because we were ahead of schedule, we took the next day off and worked in their garden. In exchange, they offered us some good meals and filled us with provisions. We left to ride the final ninety miles into Lake Tahoe.

We decided not to crank out the last ninety miles but divide it into two days, riding first to Carson City. Remember that cell phones did not yet exist, so our parents only heard from us via the occasional postcards that we would send along the way. In Carson City, I called my parents collect. It was the only time I had spoken with them since we left Indiana on May 18. I asked them if they would be willing to use their credit card to purchase a room for us at the Best Western. They agreed and we spent the final evening on the road sleeping in a comfortable bed. The Best Western gave us free coupons to play the slots. We developed a system where we put half our winnings away and were $3 ahead by early evening. In 1982, $3 could buy two McDonald's Big Macs. We splurged and had a feast with them and the provisions our friends from Fallon had provided. On June 12 we woke and rode the final thirty miles into South Lake Tahoe. We climbed up our last mountain pass between Carson City and Lake Tahoe and once we reached the top saw our first view of Lake Tahoe, a spectacular freshwater lake, with water covering 122,616 acres. To us, it looked like Holy Zion, the end of a long, arduous pilgrimage. It was finished, but like all endings, this one was another beginning, one that put us in the middle of another unknown.

Neither Bob nor I knew what came next. Bob decided to join World Impact, an urban ministry that Keith Phillips began in the 1970s as Bible studies for inner city children in Los Angeles. It then spread to Wichita, Kansas. A community house had been established in Wichita and Bob joined it. World Impact began schools and medical clinics. Its goal was to "serve the common good" in the neighborhoods where the ministry was located, which required a commitment to live in those areas. In the 1990s, The Urban Ministry Institute (TUMI) began. It "brings seminary quality education to those who live in urban neighborhoods." Bob is now the National Director of Church Planting and "Head Dean" of the Evangel School of Urban Church Planting of TUMI. As with me, his work is in theological education. His is much more practical, providing wisdom in planting and cultivating local churches by equipping indigenous leaders in those communities. Forty years of ministry with World Impact has made a significant difference in peoples' lives. Bob remained much more fully in the evangelical culture than did I, but it was an evangelical culture very different from the dominant white evangelicalism that made Trumpism viable. The vast majority of persons with whom Bob works are people of color and that social and political reality shapes a very different evangelicalism. If evangelicalism is viable post-Trump, I hope that it will be the kind of evangelicalism Bob has embodied.

MEETING RICKA IN "PRISON"

I graduated from an evangelical university, but I never regularly attended an evangelical church, having always been a United Methodist and finding myself more comfortable in Episcopal traditions. I was torn between seminary and medical school throughout my undergraduate education and applied to both my senior year. I had been placed on the waiting list for medical school but was admitted to an evangelical seminary in the northern suburbs of Chicago, and when I returned from California I decided to enroll. I drove up to find a place to live and sign up for classes, but it didn't feel right; I'm unsure why. It was too much like the world I had inhabited the past four years and I wanted to see something broader. I declined admission, returned home, and decided to take a year off while I contemplated next steps. Returning to my parents' home in Wabash, I looked for a job and found one at White's Institute, an alternative to prison for juveniles that was begun and primarily operated by the Quakers. Josiah White, a Pennsylvania Quaker and wealthy industrialist, conceived of White's Institute when he and his daughter Rebecca attended the yearly Society of Friends meeting in Indiana in 1850. White's original plan was to provide religious education according to Quaker principles for "poor children, white, colored and Indian."[10] As the founder of the Lehigh Coal and Navigation Company, he had the means to do so. He presented his plans and made financial preparation and White's Institute was established in 1850, the same year that Josiah White died.

White's Institute had undergone multiple transformations since 1850. It now serves a different group of children than when I worked there from 1982 to 1983. Then it primarily operated as an alternative to prison for juvenile offenders. It still has that role, but now focuses more on behavioral and addiction therapies. During my time there, most of the children were appointed by court order. It was exclusively residential, consisting of numerous cottages in which twenty to thirty boys or girls would live in single-sex dorms under the care of house parents, whose own families lived in the cottages with the youth. Most of the boys with whom I worked came from broken and dysfunctional families. The hope was that being part of a more normal family life might help them adjust. That many boys for one family, however, was overwhelming. The strain on family life was intense and many house parents lasted only a few years. My job was as relief house parent. I would live in the cottage and take care of the boys when the regular house parents had their days off. I worked for John and Marsha Brady, who were unusual in that they worked at White's for nearly two decades.

John had a rough upbringing, one that he continued well into early adulthood by drinking, raising hell, racing cars, and fighting anyone who wanted to fight. He was about my height—very short—but stocky and tough. He had grown up poor. Marsha grew up in a middle-class, devout Church of God family. They fell in love and got married; it was scandalous for the Church of God community in Columbia City, Indiana. John did not attend church and made no claim to Christian faith. Marsha and her mom Gladys prayed for him as they raised four young daughters. One week during a revival, Gladys asked John to join them each night. He respectfully declined, but she persisted and one night John agreed, went with them, and had an old-time conversion, radically changing his ways. He had a successful construction company at the time, was working hard and making good money, but he took seriously Jesus' command to sell everything and give it to the poor. He regularly told people about a dream he had after his conversion in which Jesus came to him and said, "Why do you have so much money in the bank when my people are hungry?" He sold the company, and he and Marsha went to work at White's Institute.

The administration at White's placed the most difficult boys with John, frequently ones with a history of violence. When they were acting out he would get in their face to see if they would back down. Despite his short stature, John could go from kind and loving to intimidating, putting the fear of God into you. In the year I worked with him, I only saw one boy refuse to back down. He was taken to prison. I visited him in jail, but he was indifferent to his situation and wanted no visitors. John gave the boys the impression that if they decided to use violence it would most likely result in a fight to the death with him; it never came to that. When John and Marsha had their days off, I was in charge of the boys. I am not intimidating and could not be if I tried. I had to discover other means to keep the boys in line, especially when they threatened each other. Only one boy hit me during the year that I worked there, and he happened to be the smallest boy, the only one I could wrestle to the ground and hold until help came.

Although it was more than a century past its Quaker origins, the Institute maintained Quaker vestiges. White's had no armed guards, barbed wire fences, or secure locks. Alarms were on doors and windows that would buzz when someone ran off, something that periodically happened. They used corporal punishment, something that did not cease until the late 1980s. It was the most difficult job that I have had in my life. The trauma most of the boys had lived through was exhausting and it took its toll on them and the people around them. House parents woke the boys for school, prepared breakfast, lined them up, and marched with them to school or chapel. The house parents were then on call in the cottage until lunch, when they would join the boys in the cafeteria, then return to the cottage in the afternoon, join them for dinner, and march with them back to the cottage for an evening routine of doing homework, playing games, going to the gym, or watching television until lights out. Although downtime was present during the day, the job prevented running or cycling because the house parent had to be on call for emergencies. What made the job difficult was not that it was physical demanding, but that it seemed so futile. Success stories were present, but they were the minority. Few boys changed or avoided the fate of a later prison sentence that seemed the inevitable path laid out for them. I marveled how John and Marsha were able to raise four daughters in that difficult setting. I married one of them.

Ricka Brady had beautiful, penetrating blue eyes. The first time I saw them, I was captivated. I still am. She is adventurous, stubborn, generous, and loyal with a great capacity for taking people in and making them feel welcome. But she does not tolerate foolishness well and will speak her mind when she sees fit. She came from a kind and loving family. She had three sisters. As I already noted, two died young. The remaining one lost a son to an automobile accident before he graduated from college. Her family has known tragedy. She had a vision early in life to be a nurse and help others through mission work. Given my own vision to be a medical doctor and work in impoverished areas, friends naturally fixed us up even before we met. We had an arranged marriage. Ricka tells people that she thought that she was marrying a doctor. I say that that she did, to which she replies, "Yes, but not that kind." Ricka's family was never opposed to education; they always supported my many years at the university. However, they did not see it as the necessity that my family did. Ricka knew that if she wanted to go to college, she would need to pay her own way. She started detasseling corn at the age of thirteen to save money for her education, something that she continued throughout her studies at Anderson University.

I jokingly tell people that I met my wife in prison. White's Institute was not really a prison; at best it could be considered a school with minimal security in place. When I began working there, Ricka was in Roatan, Honduras, an island off the north coast, running a medical clinic. Before I met her, people were telling me how much we had in common. Ricka's mother Marsha wrote her, telling her about me, and suggesting that I would be a good catch. She questioned why her mother would be trying to fix her up with their assistant house parent and was skeptical. She was in her second year of a three-year commitment in Honduras and had received a three-month furlough to return to the states and raise money for a jeep for the clinic. She was well-known on the island as a woman on a mission. Committed to seeing that the Garifuna people with whom she worked and lived had a medical clinic, she negotiated a land deal and completed all the necessary paperwork the local government required—no small task.

After we were married and living on the island, I told the mayor who my wife was, and he referred to her as a "*dura mujer*" (a tough woman). That was most likely not a compliment in his machismo culture, but I still regard it as such. Ricka's reputation grew when she confronted a neighbor who was chasing his wife with a knife. Everyone else was standing around outside, unsure what to do. She knew the couple well and knew that he did not want to harm her. She went into the house and demanded that he turn the knife over to her. He did. Perhaps that is the best of community policing. In fact, there were no police on the island, or at least none that you would call upon for assistance. Yet the place was overwhelmingly peaceful with only sporadic violence. Ricka lived through a difficult experience when another neighbor had been bludgeoned with a machete over a payment dispute. She went with him on a helicopter to the mainland, with him beaten so badly he was unrecognizable. Despite her efforts, he died. She needed a break and so she returned to the States.

I first saw her when I arrived at the cafeteria one day to collect the boys. I heard she was coming home, and many friends said we were ideal for each other. While she was skeptical about me, I was excited to meet her. I looked across the room and became entranced by her blue eyes. She looked at me and I refused to look away. We struck up a conversation as we walked with the boys back to the cottage. Shortly after that we began dating and three months later, right before she returned to Honduras, I asked her to marry me. She agreed and left the next day, spending five more months in Honduras before she returned for our wedding. I wrote her every day during those five months and she returned my letters as often as it was possible; it is how we got to know each other. Only one telephone existed on the island and every couple of weeks she would stand in line and call me. She returned to the States in mid-July and we were married two weeks later. One week after that, I returned with her to Honduras to work as a local preacher in the Caribbean Council of Methodist Churches and assist her in the clinic.

THEOLOGICAL EDUCATION

The year I married Ricka I had reapplied to medical school only to be put, once again, on the waiting list. This time I removed my name because we would be going to Honduras. I had also applied to, and been accepted at,

Duke Divinity School. I had asked my Methodist pastor where I should go to seminary and he suggested Duke. I knew nothing about it except that it had a good academic reputation and played Division 1 basketball. (They were not the powerhouse back then that they soon became.) Duke was the only school to which I applied. I was accepted and given a good scholarship, but marriage and Honduras changed my plans. I deferred for one year and left the States to spend our first year of married life on the island of Roatan in a village of the Garifuna people, an African people who had been part of the Middle Passage but rebelled from their enslaved condition and made a home on the island. They maintained African customs long after they lost memory of the precise location from which they came. Dance was a central way they told stories. Previous generations had preserved their African dialect, but only one elder still knew it, brother Toribio. He lamented that the language would die with him. The Garifuna took us in and welcomed us as if we were family.

Roatan is a beautiful island approximately forty miles long and five miles wide. It has pristine beaches and a reef that runs along the shore and attracts divers and snorkelers. When we were there, it was mired in poverty. It had no paved roads, no electricity apart from generators, no water system, and the airport runway was a dirt road next to the ocean with no lights. Planes could only come or go during daylight. Roatan has two sister islands, Utila and Guanaja. Because of British colonization, the islands had a large Methodist presence. Thirteen Methodist churches dotted the three islands. They would have services three times during the week and several times on Sunday. Local preachers were scheduled to preach on different days throughout the three islands.

When I was appointed to preach on Utila, I would have to buy passage on a shrimp boat that ran between the islands. It would take the better part of a day to make the voyage. Arriving at the island then required securing a smaller boat taxi to get to the remote Methodist churches where I would preach to a handful of people. We had one ordained elder, Rev. Austin, our "presiding elder," who was from the UK. He presided over baptisms, eucharistic celebrations, and weddings. He was a liberation theologian who wanted to transform the island into a socialist community. He led reading groups with a few of the local preachers. The first two books we read, which were the first two theology books I ever read, were Gustavo Gutiérrez's *A Theology of Liberation* and Dietrich Bonhoeffer's *The Cost of Discipleship*. I majored in chemistry at Taylor and did not have the background to make sense of either book. It would be years before I could read Gutiérrez's work with any understanding or appreciation. I was suspicious not because it was supposedly Marxist—I did not know Karl Marx from Adam Smith at that point in my life—but because it was Catholic. Bonhoeffer, I found deeply moving. His distinction between cheap and costly grace was powerful.

Rev. Austin intrigued me; growing up in rural Indiana I never met anyone like him and did not know what to make of him. Alongside working with him in the Methodist Churches, I assisted Ricka in the clinic. We provided medicine and health care at below cost, and I knew it made a difference in people's lives. But Rev. Austin suggested that free clinics like ours were part of the problem rather than the solution. Run primarily as a charity sponsored from funds and visiting medical teams from the United States, it forestalled the medical crisis that would require the government to attend to the health of its citizens. I thought there was something to what he said. The health issues we saw daily resulted from infrastructure failures like a lack of clean water and sanitation. We did not have the resources to address these lacks. We were attending to symptoms, not the underlying problems. Nonetheless, people still needed blood pressure medicine, women gave birth and needed care, and people were sick and would potentially die without attention. I could point to individuals in the village who were alive because of Ricka's nursing skills.

Most baby deliveries were attended by midwives; only the difficult births would be brought to the clinic and I witnessed Ricka successfully deliver them. We did not have adequate painkillers; my only role was to hold the woman so that she would not come off the table at the most painful moments. Although I found Rev. Austin's criticisms worthy of consideration, I could not will the crisis that would cause the revolutionary changes he desired. He was right about the need for political and infrastructure change, and much of the charity doled out had more to do with salving the conscience of the giver than addressing the underlying problems. Ricka and I attempted to make the clinic part of the village. We created a board of villagers who would make decisions on how much should be charged for medicine so that it could become self-supporting. The US evangelical mission that operated the clinic caught wind of it and required us to disband the board.

Rev. Austin charged me with working at a church in French Harbor. The island was composed of white persons of British descent, Black Caribs or the Garifuna, and mestizos who settled there from the mainland. On the whole, people got along and worked together. But there were tensions. The predominantly white church in French Harbor had not reached out to the growing Black presence and Rev. Austin tasked me with leading that effort. I would lead the Wednesday and Thursday evening worship services. French Harbor was 9.8 miles from Punta Gorda, where we lived. Taxis ran inconsistently along the single road that covered the length of the island. We had, for a time, a beat-up Land Rover that occasionally ran. It lacked a battery and had one working brake. I parked it on a hill and would pop the clutch to start it. Once when transporting a visiting team, I parked on the hill leading down into the water when the remaining brake failed; the vehicle started to roll with no way to stop. There were only two options: plunge into the water with a jeep filled with people or head into a coconut tree. It was not quite the trolley problem used in some ethics courses, where a trolley's brakes go out and a bystander can decide to turn the trolley to save five people by killing fewer than that. I've never found that way of teaching ethics through exceptional dilemmas compelling. Rolling down that hill toward the water provided little time for calculative reasoning. I hoped I could steer the Land Rover into a coconut tree without harming my passengers. We hit the tree and it stopped the vehicle. Everyone was unharmed. We bent the bumper off the wheel, fixed the one salvageable brake, and continued to drive the jeep until it finally died. After that, we no longer had a vehicle to drive, but we did have a classic Chinese bicycle, something like the "flying pigeon" well known as the egalitarian form of transportation in the People's Republic. I have no idea how that bicycle made its way to Punta Gorda, but it was the only thing I had to ride. It was heavy and durable, and I would sometimes ride it over the dirt roads to French Harbor for my preaching engagements. Overall, cycling and running were infrequent during this year, but walking was ever present. We seemed always to be walking to some destination in the hot Caribbean sun.

Ricka and I returned to the United States in the summer of 1984, moved to Durham, North Carolina, and I began seminary at Duke Divinity School. I was still considering medical school, but first wanted to study theology and become a Methodist minister. I found my calling studying theology. Stanley Hauerwas moved from Notre Dame to Duke to teach Christian ethics the same year I matriculated, and I was assigned along with my good friend David Matzko McCarthy as his advisee. Stanley had to sign off on our proposed coursework. He looked at mine and asked why I wasn't taking more courses in theology; the well-known theologian Geoffrey Wainwright was offering a graduate seminar on the doctrine of the Trinity and Stanley advised that I take it rather than a course in pastoral counseling. The latter was required for ordination, but I decided to follow Hauerwas's advice and forego that course for Wainwright's seminar. Little did I know that his counsel would set me in a new vocational direction.

Hauerwas was as enigmatic to me as had been Rev. Austin. His rough language coupled with strong convictions about nonviolence seemed antithetical to each other. His Christian ethics course disoriented me. As an evangelical, I was drawn to the correlation between Christology and ethics, but his emphasis on the church seemed too Catholic, too influenced by his years at Notre Dame. I grew up not far from that university, and always considered it an elitist import into northern Indiana for wealthy Catholic kids from the Chicago suburbs. My father was a Purdue graduate, and we frequently went to the Purdue-Notre Dame football game. For me, Purdue was the real Indiana school, the school of the people. Notre Dame might as well have been in Rome. Here I was at a Methodist seminary, learning about the church from a former Notre Dame professor who brought with him several Notre Dame students who eventually became my close friends. Unsure what to make of Hauerwas's ethics, I would take long bicycle rides in the afternoon and think through his lectures and the correlative reading. Eventually, it began to make sense and I discovered a satisfying form of Christianity that replaced the individualism of my evangelical past.

The next seven years were busy with graduate school and children, but also provided more opportunity for cycling than living in Roatan. I joined my first cycling club, Bull City Cycling, and learned much from its members that I did not know in my previous years of solo riding in rural Indiana. As a cyclist, I was an anomaly in rural Indiana in the early 1980s. The film *Breaking Away* came out in 1979 and had a significant impact in promoting cycling. There is a scene where Dave, the working-class Indiana kid who takes up cycling and longs to be like the Italians, shaves his legs while his father looks on horrified. Shaving legs is a sign of crossing over into serious cycling; it observes Velominati rule # 33, "shave your guns." Pros do it to make their post-race massage easier, but few cyclists are pros and nearly all serious cyclists shave their legs. Other reasons for shaved legs are that it makes removing the debris from road rash easier or is more aerodynamic when riding. Unless you are a pro or serious racer, however, those reasons are little more than excuses to justify the real reason cyclists shave their legs: they want to look like serious cyclists. If you roll up to another cyclist and want to determine how serious they are, you can check out their kit, their bike, or give them the highest level of scrutiny and see if their legs are shaven. Shaved legs are part of the gestalt of cycling. I began shaving mine so I would look like the other guys riding with Bull City Cycling. Ricka was never convinced about the merits of my shaven legs so we came up with a compromise. I would shave them between Easter and Thanksgiving and cease doing so from Thanksgiving to Easter.

COMMUTING AND THE VIRTUES
AND VICES OF CYCLING

Our time in seminary was rich in friendship but kept us near the poverty line. We could barely afford one car, purchasing one without air conditioning in hot, humid North Carolina. I had my bicycle and began commuting out of necessity in 1984. As a longtime cyclist-commuter, my anecdotal evidence is that automobile drivers have become more tolerant of cyclists on the road. I wonder if it is due to the reality of climate change. Back in the early eighties, drivers would often hurl insults or threats your way. Commuting along a very safe road in Durham, an old white guy in a truck pulled up next to me, rolled down his window, and with a serious look on his face said, "Boy, you better git off these roads or I'ma gonna wear you as a hood ornament." Fortunately, he then sped off. Out of the multitude of angry encounters with motorists over the years, I distinctly remember that one because I thought it was at least creative. I've seldom had bad encounters in rural Indiana where I often ride in the summers when I'm visiting my parents' lake cabin. I wonder if it has to do with farm culture and the many tractors that are on the roads slowing down cars, or maybe the occasional Amish buggy. People seem accustomed to something other than cars speeding along the rural roads. I have also found Milwaukee and the surrounding areas accommodating of cyclists. Perhaps it is due to the bicycle manufacture Trek's influence; Trek's headquarters is located in Wisconsin and they host an annual ride, the Trek 100, which has always been a favorite. Trek supports cycling throughout Wisconsin. My worst encounters occurred in two very different places, Evanston, Illinois and Philadelphia, Pennsylvania.

Evanston would appear to be a safe place to bicycle with its idyllic homes along Sheridan Road, and on the whole I found it a decent place to ride. To encourage cycling, Evanston put European bike lanes along Sheridan Road, which runs adjacent to Northwestern University. These lanes are marked off from the road and have their own traffic control lights for cyclists. I've ridden on similar bike lanes in Switzerland and Germany where drivers are accustomed to giving cyclists their right of way; they are fantastic, but European bike lanes with American drivers are not always a good mix. Motorists must be accustomed to checking the bike lane before turning into it. The bike lane is to the right of the motorist, marked off by some kind of barrier. When an intersection occurs where the motorist can make a right turn, the barrier gives way and the car and bicycle potentially share the same space. American drivers are unaccustomed to looking to their right before turning right. Drivers might pass a cyclist and then without looking turn back into them. In cycling lingo, this is known as a "right hook" and is something that cyclists must be aware of, along with being "doored," if they are not to be a motorist's casualty.

On two occasions in Evanston, luxury SUVs gave me a right hook, forcing me to hit the brakes as forcefully as I could. A sudden stop like that can throw you over your handlebars or make you lose control of your bike. Adrenaline started pumping and I confess that I yelled at the driver, "What the hell are you doing? You have to give me my right of way. You could have killed me." The first time it happened, a woman retorted, "I didn't hit you, did I? Why are you getting loud with me?" I yelled back, "You only didn't hit me because I watched out for you." Her son flipped me off, only fueling my anger at their lack of concern for my safety. Such encounters have the potential not to end well. They are best avoided, but the adrenaline takes over and tempts toward intemperance. I rode off, fuming at their injustice. One week later at the exact same spot, a different luxury SUV made the same unthoughtful maneuver. I hit the brakes again, felt the adrenaline, and said something similar. "Oh, I'm so sorry," said the woman driving the SUV. "It was my fault. I was not looking. I'll remember to do so next time." "Thank you," I replied, embarrassed that I had raised my voice.

Thirteen blissful miles of commuting in Philly culminated in two miles of terror when I arrived in Manayunk and turned onto Green Lane to take the bridge over the river into the city. It was barely wide enough for the automobile traffic and motorists resented a cyclist taking up space. One day a large truck gave me no room. I swear I could feel the paint from his truck on my shoulder as he came as close as he could even though he had space to move over. It had to be intentional. I learned early on that it is counterproductive for a cyclist to flip motorists off, but I did raise my hands up as if to say, "What is your deal?" He saw it in his mirror and had had enough. Brakes squealed, the truck lurch to a stop, blocking traffic, and a mountain of a man jumped out of the truck walking aggressively toward me, calling me a "sonavabitch." My first thought was, "This is going to hurt."

I had been in situations like this before but had always been able to find an escape route. A large man in his work clothes and boots is not able to catch me on my bike if I have even a slight head start. This time, no escape route was available. The traffic had me pinned in as drivers from the City of Brotherly Love began honking at the man; I think more because he had stopped traffic unnecessarily than because he was threatening me. He was indifferent to their pleas and stompingly continued toward me. Wanting to avoid his balled-up fists, I began to apologize, "I'm sorry, sir, if my actions caused you any trouble or offense." I don't know if the apology caught him off guard, if he saw how small I was and decided it better not to pummel me in public, or if the honking cars caused him to change his mind, but he stopped, hurled a few more invectives my way, returned to his truck, and drove off. I was relieved but ashamed. I am not above apologizing, but I had not done anything improper. Apologizing out of fear seemed cowardly.

My cowardice troubled me because cycling, and especially commuting, was a practice that I imagined developed the virtue of courage. As an ethicist, I study and teach about the virtues and often ask students where they learn virtue. Answers have been consistent over the years: family, religious institutions, participation in sports teams or in the orchestra, among friends. I've thought that cycling, especially commuting and riding with friends, cultivates virtues. Riding a bicycle on roads makes you vulnerable to drivers and all manner of hazards. It was one of the few places in my life that required physical courage. Courage faces fear with neither cowardice nor recklessness. Sharing a road with motorists, on roads that are less than ideal, and riding with other cyclists, can be fear-inducing. Crashing and breaking bones prompts reconsideration of riding. The first time I rode after a broken collar bone set me on edge. Prior to that event, I had no firsthand knowledge what crashing could do. I was oblivious to the negative impact cycling could have on the body; now I would always know those impacts were a possibility. It took some time to feel comfortable on the bike without the hesitation that fear brings. Eventually, riding develops confidence that sets the possibility of crashing out of mind; it can create recklessness, a feeling of invulnerability, which tempts cyclists to do stupid things. I have done such and was saved from myself by kind motorists who were looking out for me when I was not looking out for myself. Courage is not recklessness; it is an appropriate response to fear.

Moderating fear also requires temperance. Long-distance cycling itself may not cultivate the virtue of temperance; it is an extreme form of activity. When I asked my cardiologist if I would be able to cycle like I did prior to the implantation of the pacemaker, his response was "within moderation." I was unsure what that meant. I spent decades pushing my limits, attempting new distance, speed, and elevation records. Had I lived intemperately? Although long-distance activities push the boundary of what appears to be temperate, they also require practices of temperance in order to sustain them—practices such as eating well, getting sufficient sleep, maintaining one's physical and emotional health, avoiding excess in all kinds of pleasures, and learning to endure suffering. Suffering, Paul tells us, produces endurance, which in turn produces character and character hope (Romans 5:3–4). Of course, he did not have cycling or athletics in mind when he wrote those words. Nonetheless, cycling has the possibility of producing character and hope through the ability to endure. It moderates some desires for the ability to ride over a lifetime. And yet, I write this after a heart failure, which may have been exacerbated by years of pushing my heart to its limits. It is unclear if my cycling harmed or helped my situation.

I have asked each cardiologist that has attended me if they thought my long-distance activities contributed to my heart failure. That question preoccupied me at first. It is not unusual. The authors of *The Haywire Heart* comment on how many long-distance athletes who have cardiac incidents are likewise preoccupied with this question. I've thought a great deal about why. One reason is the desire to know if we have been unwise, if what we thought was a salutary practice was in fact harming us. A second reason has to do with control. If we somehow contributed to our heart failure, we might still have some control over our lives, a control that may very well be illusory. Which answer would be preferable, to know that nothing I could have done would have prevented this or to know that had I lived otherwise I could have avoided it? The first suggests that no matter what we do, the contingencies of life can undo it; the second that changes in our live can prevent undesired contingencies. It gives us a sense of control, and perhaps to control our destiny lets us live virtuously. But virtue is not control; it is learning to live well given the contingencies each of us inevitably face. It is the practical wisdom of knowing how to make the best of a situation with the right disposition directed toward appropriate ends in the right way at the right time. Virtue does not flee from the fragility of life but receives it without being destroyed by it. To that end, cycling can be a form of practical wisdom.

Cycling generates technical skills; it is less clear if it produces practical wisdom. Technical skills do not involve persons in ways of living that make them virtuous. A person can be an excellent cyclist but a terrible human being. They might know when to attack, how to attack, and have the power to attack in a race or even on a friendly ride. Perhaps their love of cycling is for the fleeting glory of honor in victory? They view other cyclists as competitors to be destroyed rather than friends with whom one cooperates. If cycling cultivates practical wisdom it would have to be other than this.

Cycling can be a cooperative form of activity by which people ride together to achieve a common end. Take for instance a pace line. It occurs when a small number of riders decide to cooperate. Two lines are formed. Depending on wind direction, one line will ride one mile per hour slower than the other. If you are riding north and there is a northeast wind, the right side of the pace line would be slower because the slower side would do less work, using less power into the wind. Cyclists on the left side are shielded from the wind; they ride a bit faster. The two sides constantly rotate. When a rider becomes the last rider on the slow side, they move into the faster left side, passing the riders on the right, moving to the front and then rotating to the right, slowing down again. If everyone cooperates well, no one is riding hard into the wind except for a few seconds each rotation. When everyone knows how to do it well, it is a beautiful thing to participate in, like a finely tuned instrument.

Riding a pace line takes practical skill. The point is to make smooth transitions from the slow to the fast line and then back to the slow line, maintaining as tight a formation as possible. It is an incredibly efficient way to ride. Cyclists unaccustomed to it often make mistakes by turning it into a competition, riding too fast in the fast lane, and wrongly thinking that the task is to get to the front as quickly as possible. Another common mistake is to fail to slow down adequately when moving into the slow lane, forcing the rider behind to use too much energy to pass when they arrive at the front. The technical skills in riding a pace line are not necessarily virtuous but learning to cooperate in a common endeavor to ride as efficiently as possible can be. Accomplished riders discover how to do the right thing in the right way at the right time in order that everyone flourishes. Any practice that accomplishes such an end brings with it virtues of cooperation, generosity, and friendship that extend beyond cycling into everyday life.

Virtues overlap. The generosity and friendship that arise from the practical wisdom intrinsic to cooperative activities are necessary for justice. It is a virtue of order or harmony that allows us to render obligations to each other that we owe as people who must learn to live in solidarity. Justice arises from ordering life together toward common goods and loves, whether that be as a cycling club, a family, a neighborhood, a village or town, city, state, nation, or church. Worship has traditionally been placed under the virtue of justice. We owe God worship and by worshipping God we fulfill a duty. Essential to the proper ordering of life together is the possibility of free movement. Perhaps nothing has been more essential and neglected as a practice of justice than transportation; free movement on roads may be one of the last remaining commons where we learn to live together. The consequences of not doing so lead to deep injustices and harms.

In a famous, or infamous, 1968 essay, Garrett Hardin described the "tragedy of the commons" as one of the central problems of shared, communal resources. If everyone has access to a common resource without individual accountability, then it is possible for one person to use more than their share of the resource, draining the commons of its shared value. It also makes possible "free riders" who use the shared commons without contributing to it. Capitalist economists frequently identify the tragedy of the commons as one of the central problems of socialism. Communally owned property cannot work because free riders and individuals will not be required to exercise the thrift necessary for a sustainable order. Dividing the commons up, turning it into private property, and making owners responsible for their property supposedly allocate resources more efficiently than the collective responsibility necessary for common ownership. In his work, *The Invention of Capitalism: Classical Political Economy and the Secret History of Primitive Accumulation*, Michael Perelman traces the history of the rise of capitalism through the private accumulation of what were once understood to be commons through enclosures and private ownership. He asks the question, what would motivate someone to move from working on common land as a farmer and hunter into Adam Smith's pin-making factory where they sell their labor to the owner and are content to do nothing each day for hours but one operation involved in making pins. Smith began his 1776 *Wealth of Nations* with the pin-making factory as an example of efficient production. He assumes it is natural without asking the question Perelman asks. For Smith, the pin-making factory just is. It exists without a history. Perelman tells us the history behind its origin.

Commons have largely disappeared. Since the 1970s, a concerted political and economic effort occurred to extract profit from the commons by privatizing it as much as possible. The result has been a marked increase in global inequality and a loss of common spaces and resources. If justice is a virtue of order or harmony that teaches us to live together well, then this ideological trend diminishes the ability to live into that virtue. It assumes that constructing our political and economic existence through self-interest will have the unexpected consequences of promoting harmony more so than trying to live justly. Cycling has the potential to challenge this ideology, tacitly and explicitly. It does so because it requires people to share one of the last remaining forms of the commons that still exists, and is necessary for everyday life—roads.

Over the past four decades of cycling, one trend that encourages me is the number of places in cities, villages, and rural areas that place signs by the side of the road with an image of the bicycle that says, "Share the Road." It is a small thing but consider how rare it is to be encouraged to share goods in common in our society. No one entering a bank is challenged with a sign that reads, "Share the Wealth," or into a government building to find one that says, "Share the Power," or in a hospital with a reminder, "Share Health Care Resources." Because these places are not assumed to be commons but private accumulations of wealth or power, an encouragement to share would be perplexing. Roads, however, are still common, at least in most places.

Numerous historical, political, cultural, and sociological works have emerged in the past two decades questioning the dominance of the car and asking how the bicycle could restructure our common life to make for more sustainable, livable, and just communities. As a forty-year commuter who has lived in five different cities during that time, I have discovered that commuting requires you to ask different questions about something as basic as where your live and its relation to roads. Is your home within range of a safe cycling commute? I've also discovered that the answers to that question vary. In my thirties, a fifteen-mile commute was acceptable. It was reduced to ten in my forties, then seven in my fifties, and now I have a leisurely two-mile commute. This question, of course, is not the only one or even the most important that bicycle commuting raises. Perhaps a more important one is how we learn to share a necessary resource for life together—the road. James Longhurst's *Bike Battles: A History of Sharing the American Road* is an important work that places the bicycle in its historical and social context in the US. His conclusion is titled, "The Road as a Commons," and despite his book's title, his point is that "battle" is seldom the appropriate term for the contests that occur over a necessary shared resource. He writes, "Thinking of the road as a commons highlights the problems of overuse and managing competing demands, but it also reminds us that comparable common-pool resources have been managed perfectly well."[11] The commons can be tragic. When that happens on our roadways, cyclists bear its brunt. In a contest between an automobile and a bicycle, the bicycle always loses. Yet, what is surprising is how seldom these conflicts occur. The negative encounters I have had with automobiles that were not the result of my own carelessness are surprisingly small given the amount of time that I have spent on the road the past forty years. On the whole, people take collective responsibility for each other. Sharing the road produces the justice of living together in harmony. This collective responsibility may also indicate the charity of providence. We are placed in situations where the best course of action is to cooperate and be generous with each other.

Not everyone, of course, is satisfied with the just, collective responsibility necessary for a shared resource. Longhurst notes that when bike lanes were first proposed in New York City, one person opposed them in an editorial, writing that they signified "an invasion of socialist-leaning, Eurocentric, limp-wristed Lycra warriors."[12] Why it is somehow more courageous to hide behind 2,400 pounds of steel than making yourself a vulnerable user of the road perplexes me. In the first edition of his *Naked Economics*, Charles Wheelan defended buying the largest vehicle possible as a rational economic decision to secure his family against the potential hazards that arise when one ventures onto the roadways. Rather than viewing the road as a common resource, he viewed it as a war of all against all where one must protect oneself at the expense of others. Such a sentiment is self-defeating. If Wheelan is correct, then each driver would be responsible for purchasing bigger and bigger vehicles to secure their life. To his credit, Wheelan revised his unjust claim in later editions of the book. It does not teach us to live well together, but to live at the expense of each other.

Roads make possible freedom of movement. I am able to get on my bicycle in Milwaukee or Dallas and ride through neighborhoods, villages, subdivisions, and urban centers without, on the whole, paying tolls or special assessments to do so. In the 1890s, before the invention of the automobiles when roads were dirt paths overseen by local authorities, bicycles were designated vehicles with a right to the road along with horses, carriages, pedestrians, and other vehicles in the US. Roads were a mixed-use commons. It could have been otherwise. Freedom of movement could be restricted. I cannot ride from the northern US into Canada or from the southern US into Mexico. These are not natural boundaries but politically imagined ones.

In 2010 I had a sabbatical in Basel, Switzerland to do research on two theologians who were friends, the Protestant Karl Barth and the Catholic Hans Urs von Balthasar. I took my bicycle for transportation and would ride in the afternoon for exercise.

My Trek 5200 outside Karl Barth's home, where his archives reside.

I would accidentally ride into Germany and France and not know it except for changes in the language in road signs because the borders were not policed. The European Union meant freedom of movement without requiring me to show papers. How different those days were than when my great uncle was a prisoner of war in Germany. Freedom of movement is one of the greatest and most precarious freedoms. Restrictions can easily become irrational. The four miles between Laredo, Texas and Nuevo Laredo, Mexico become more difficult to travel than the 2,000-plus miles from Laredo to Portland, Oregon or Portland, Maine, even though people between the two Laredos depend upon each other in a way that people between the two Portlands do not. Imagine, however, if I marked out the road in front of my home, set up a toll booth, and charged persons to pass through. We do not permit this because travel has been a protected activity since medieval times. The English term *highway* goes back to the twelfth century; its original meaning stated that it was a path available to anyone to travel. We see this understanding still present in our reference to roads as "freeways." They are supported by taxes, but it is assumed that everyone should have access to them independent of the taxes that they pay.

Cycling, especially commuting, is one way to perpetuate the justice of sharing a common resource, but cycling is not an intrinsically just activity. Although it began as a way to democratize transportation, making it more egalitarian, and there are places where it still functions as such, as a leisure-time activity cycling emerges out of economic inequality. Not everyone has the surplus income required for it. Cycling is expensive. The original penny-farthing bicycle of the late nineteenth century cost $125, which was seven months' salary for a farm laborer. The "safety bicycle" developed at the end of that century was more affordable. It was one of the first mass-marketed items. In the mid 1890s, three million were produced for a country of sixty-three million people. The penny-farthing was elitist and ridden by groups who practiced social exclusions based on class, race, and gender. In 1894 the League of American Wheelmen (LAW) explicitly excluded Blacks from its organization. It barred Major Taylor, one of America's first and greatest competitive cyclists, from belonging to the primary organization for cyclists. LAW sanctioned US races, excluding him from many. These elitist groups required a specific dress to show cycling was done by gentlemen of note, but the twentieth century saw the loss of elitist society riding bicycles. They were replaced by golf. The cheaper safety bicycle made it possible for diverse classes to purchase one and that diminished its status as a class distinction.[13]

Although cycling is more evenly distributed along class lines today, making commuting possible for a wide variety of people, competitive cycling remains an overwhelmingly white and expensive pastime. Justin Williams is a rare individual, a Black professional cyclist who grew up in South Los Angeles. Cycling provided a way out of the tough neighborhood where he grew up. Despite his racing success, he had difficulty find a supporting team. He explains, "I was written off faster than other riders and watched a lot of guys get on teams that never won a race. As a Black man from the 'hood, I was typecast before managers even got to know me." He began his own cycling team, L39ION, "Legion," to address the racial injustices in cycling. It includes partnering with a nonprofit, "Outride," that encourages cycling for poorer riders. Competitive cycling is changing for the better. The US professional team Education First (EF) recently initiated cycling programs at two HBCUs (historically Black colleges and universities) in response to the Black Lives Matter movement.[14] Businesses like "Dream Bikes" in Milwaukee recycle good used bicycles, making them available to people without the means to purchase such bikes new. If the road is to be a common resource, and the bicycle a means to traverse it freely, then access must be more justly distributed.

Cycling fosters courage, encourages temperance, requires practical wisdom, and can inculcate justice. These four virtues are known as the "cardinal virtues." Since antiquity, they have been recognized as a "hinge," from the Latin *cardo*, by which one lives well in the world. Cycling can be a virtuous activity. Whether it is or not is not the most pressing reason for why someone rides a bicycle. No one sets out riding by asking the question, how can I be a virtuous person? That is not surprising. People seldom set out to be virtuous by concentrating explicitly on being virtuous. Directly pursuing a virtuous life could produce a self-absorption that works against a virtuous life. It is tantamount to taking great pride in one's humility. Virtue is more of a surprising gift than an achievement, which is why the theological virtues of faith, hope, and love are said to be "infused." They are worked by God in us. We receive them as gifts rather than acquire them through our own inner resources.

IT'S ABOUT THE RIDE

Cycling cultivates a disposition to power your body through space for diverse ends—to get to work, to enjoy time with friends, to compete against others, to contemplate nature, to gain health, to rehab from previous injuries, to maintain weight, to lessen a carbon footprint, and more. In the end, however, cycling is about riding the bike; it's about the ride and rides take different forms. Most cycling clubs have standing rides that provide consistent possibilities for their members. The Spokesmen meet at a fountain in

Wauwatosa at 5:45 AM every Tuesday, Thursday, and Friday for a fifteen- to twenty-mile ride. Mark, Jason, Frederick, and Phil are regulars. It has a normal route to Lake Michigan and back, often arriving at the lake as the sun begins to rise, and followed by coffee and conversation.

The aesthetics of the morning ride are as motivating as the ride itself. A few members of the Mirage Cycling Club meet at White Rock Lake in Dallas at 6:00 AM, Monday through Friday. Tommy, Josh, Jeroen, Christopher, and Phillip are regulars. If someone does not make it on time, they ride counterclockwise and flash their lights to signal they are looking for their friends. The club usually makes two laps around the lake; the first is in the dark and on the second, the sun rises, making for spectacular views. Beginning a ride in the dark and watching the sun rise is a deeply satisfying way to greet the new day. Riding regularly with others does much more than produce fitness; it creates friendship.

The Spokesmen are unique as a cycling club. It began in the 1980s when three gentlemen, Bob, Joe, and Dan, purchased bicycles together in order to receive a discount. Having purchased bikes, they felt a need to ride them to justify the costs to their wives. They had no desire to race or compete, but to get together for leisure rides for the sake of friendship. They were intentional about this purpose, discussing how difficult it can be for middle-aged men to befriend one another and spend time together. Riding provided the occasion to gather and cultivate friendship. They invited others to join them, and Jon decided that they should have a common kit. This required a name and thus the "Spokesmen" were born. Regular riding times were established, and anyone could join with the one proviso that they had to be a safe rider.

The Spokesmen have no dues; nor do they have a membership form. They have a website and an email list. If someone seeks to join, they send in a request and the list administrator, a purely voluntary job, asks if anyone can vouch for the potential member's safe riding skills. No one cares how fast or slow anyone rides. What matters is safety. Once someone vouches for them, then they are invited to be Spokesmen and are placed on the email list, which is only to be used for cycling-related matters. The Spokesmen rides can be challenging; the club is not for people who are out of shape or seldom bicycle, but the rides are never beatdowns. The unstated but central rule is that how we ride together must contribute to friendship. Cyclists can race up hills or have serious exertions that break up the group, but then they must wait for each other and ride at a pace that keeps everyone together. The one exception to keeping together is the Thursday morning "puker" ride. Given its name because early on a rider hurled at the top of it, the puker is a .2-mile hill at 5 percent grade followed by a .4 mile downhill that circles around to the start of the hill. Riders begin together, yet it is understood that each should do the hill repeats at their own speed. Some riders do twelve to fifteen hill repeats; others do thirty or more. It is an excellent workout that deserves its name and is also followed by gathering at a local coffee shop.

The Spokesmen are much more than a cycling club. They gather together for annual celebrations, including the much anticipated "movie night" at Steve Longo's house. He caters a meal in his backyard and always features some movie about cycling. The Spokesmen also go for easy weekend jaunts that include camping or hotel overnights. They support one another well. When they heard about my cardiac episode, I was inundated with inquiries and well-wishes. They have also suffered accidents together; it inevitably happens. I contributed to one such incident in which one of my favorite riders, David, broke his collar bone. David is a tall, strong rider with explosive power. We have ridden many long, multiday rides together. On long climbs, he has the ability to take off sprinting, leaving riders in his wake; it is beautiful to watch the power he can put out. I've tried to stay with him in these explosive outbursts, but after many times riding with him, I learned that I cannot do it without paying too steep a price. Not even he can sustain that power on a long climb. My only hope to stay with him is to elevate the pace slightly and ride a consistent pace slowly attempting to pull myself up to him. He often then takes off with that same explosive power.

On one Spokesmen ride, we had a fairly strong crew, and we were pushing a strong pace. It was my turn at the front; we were clipping along when I heard someone yelling from the back that we had missed a turn. I thought everyone heard it, and I eased up ever so slightly. When you are riding at the front, you never ease up without warning the rider behind you by putting down your hand. I made no signal and the rider behind me (Bill) touched my wheel. He went down hard, but as is often the case, it was the rider behind Bill, who happened to be David, who took the brunt of the accident. He flipped over Bill's bike, slamming into the road and breaking his collar bone. I felt horrible. Spokesmen are forgiving and Bill and David remain my close friends.

When I had a sabbatical in Los Angeles, my good friend Jon, a fellow Spokesman, came out to visit and we rode some of the classic LA rides together, Highway 1 and deep into the San Gabriel mountains. After we moved to Dallas, Jon came down and rode the South Loop and more with me. Brien and Jim also found their way to Dallas at different times. They rented bicycles and I introduced them to riding at White Rock Lake. Cycling brings people together. I have made it a habit at professional meetings, if possible, to take an afternoon and go for a ride often with others by renting a bicycle at a local shop. When the Society of Christian Ethics met in

Portland, my former student and friend Ben Suriano, who lived in the area, joined with me for several rides. When the American Academy of Religion met in Denver, two fellow theologians, Peter Dula and Chris Huebner, invited me to come up one day early and meet them in Boulder to ride the "Left Hand Canyon," a classic training ride for pros that takes riders up to the Continental Divide. We descended in snow, which made me nervous but Chris, being from Canada, displayed amazing descent skills through the patches of snow that were still present on the road.

Weekend rides tend to be longer and begin later. They vary based on the time of year and the level of fitness. Coming out of winter into spring in Wisconsin often finds riders in less-than-ideal shape. Perhaps they rode indoors, skied cross-country, or rode slow maintenance rides in the snow and ice. Dallas riders tend to stay fit year-round; something I discovered in making the transition from six weeks of winter riding in Wisconsin back to Texas in mid-January and finding myself struggling to keep up with the Mirage riders. Regular rides create bonds of friendship because riders spend a great deal of time together. When the pace is fast, conversations lag as the group of riders strings out single file doing all they can to hold the wheel of the person in front of them. When the pace lessens, conversation occurs.

Josh's long rides on Saturday in Dallas with a limited number of other riders are among my favorites. Like me, Josh likes to go long. Unlike me, Josh is fast. He throws out a route before a Saturday South Loop, inviting people to turn off at some point on the South Loop and join him for a 100-plus route. The South Loop can have up to fifty riders on it; it is difficult to get to know people given the numbers and speed. Josh will do the first twenty to thirty miles of the South Loop at a fast pace and then turn off with a few riders for a longer ride, spending most of his time at the front riding a consistent twenty-plus mph pace; he is as smooth as butter. He does not mind that I stick to his wheel and only take a few pulls. His rides are for smaller groups in which, unlike the South Loop, riders get to know one another.

Because most of my regular cycling companions know what I do for a living, I have heard confessions, discussed faith or the reasons for the lack thereof, and had interesting conversations about ethics and politics. Of course, such conversations can be controversial. In fact, as a university professor, most of my academic colleagues have a similar political outlook, albeit not so much a religious one. Cycling brought me in conversation with a wider range of political and religious views. As a religious person and minister, many if not most of my closest friends are people who share faith. My closest secular friends are cyclists. I have learned a great deal from them.

Then there are special annual rides. One such ride is the famous "Bone Ride" that starts in Wauwatosa, heads eighty miles west to Madison, Wisconsin for lunch, and then returns as a full-on race back to Wauwatosa, making for a 160-mile day. The Bone Ride was featured in *Bicycling* magazine in 2013 under the title, "Down to the Bone: When A Ride Is Hard Enough to Make You Question Who You Are, You Might Not Like The Answer You Get."[15] The ride begins at the home of Tom Schuler, a US national road racing champion and member of the 7-Eleven cycling team. I have the good fortune of living a few blocks from his home, so unlike many Bone Riders who came from some distance, I rolled out of bed, put on my cycling gear, and rode a few blocks to line up with the more than 100 riders who join together the third week in May for an early season beatdown. The Bone Ride is not advertised; it is not a sanctioned ride. There is a sag wagon that drives behind cyclists, picking up any that find themselves in difficulty due to being out of shape or having mechanical problems. There is no police escort. Riders discover the Bone Ride by word of mouth.

Schuler rode this route to train during his days with the 7-Eleven professional cycling team. Someone told him that was a "boneheaded" method of training and thus the ride received its name. The ride to Madison is moderately paced. The large peloton breaks up into three or four groups of twenty to thirty riders, spaced out so that cars can pass safely. Riders ride two by two, maintaining twenty mph. It is quick and steady but does not put seasoned cyclists under pressure. Schuler insists that the pace be maintained; no one tries to break away or elevate the pace without incurring the wrath of the group. There are no stops during the four hours that it takes to ride the first eighty miles. No one is going to slow down for riders who stop for a "natural." They are on their own to regain the peloton, which is not easy at its speed of twenty mph.

Cyclists arrive in Madison and take over the various restaurants as they sit and chat, primarily discussing cycling. Then they gather en masse about one hour later and begin the ride back, starting with a slow roll through the city of Madison until the large single peloton, which has now swelled in size having picked up other riders along the way, approaches a significant hill on the outskirts of the city and the race is on. For the remainder of the final seventy-five miles, riders push as hard as they are able. The moderately paced ride turns into an arduous challenge. The riders have no need to break up into groups because the acceleration from the faster riders sheds cyclists right and left as groups of riders with similar capabilities find each other, riding a pace line through the Wisconsin countryside back to Wauwatosa.

My first Bone Ride filled me with excitement and fear. The most I had ridden in a single day prior to it was 140 miles, but it was at a leisurely pace.

I trained for the Bone Ride, but I was uncertain how I would handle it. I woke up early, rode to Schuler's house as cyclists gathered, and sensed the nervous energy among them. Riding in a large group of unfamiliar riders causes stress. How seasoned are the riders surrounding you? Are they newbies taking on a challenge beyond their skill level, always a potential hazard? We had some anxious moments on the way out. A cardinal sin when riding in a group is to overlap wheels with the person in front. A rider should remain directly behind the rider in front, or slightly to the right or left based on wind direction. The rider in front might not be aware where the rider behind is. If they overlap wheels and the front rider pulls off or is required to make a slight adjustment due to something in the road, then they can touch wheels, causing the rider behind to crash. As happened to my friend David, it will be the riders behind the one who touches wheels that will most likely bear the consequences of a rider's misjudgment. Sure enough, a rider to my left overlapped wheels with the lead rider. When he pulled off to the left to let another take his place they almost crashed. Brakes were pressed as a quick slowdown took place, something that you want to avoid when riding in a group at high speeds. Fortunately, no one went down. The errant cyclist was admonished.

A woman riding to my right on a triathlon bike and I begin a conversation. Triathletes and road cyclists are like ranchers and farmers. Velominati rule 42 states, "A bike race shall *never* be preceded with a swim and/or followed with a run." Triathletes ride alone so they are unaccustomed to riding in a group. They also have tri-bars in the center of the handlebars that make for a more efficient way of riding but at the expense of control. Triathletes who place their hands on tri-bars during a group ride will soon hear about it from road cyclists riding with them. Triathletes, however, like to ride at the front of a paceline for extended periods of time. Race the Lake around Lake Winnebago in Wisconsin is an annual ninety-five-mile race that begins in waves based on riders' abilities. Triathletes are not allowed to begin until wave three. I once raced it with them, started in wave three, and had a triathlete pull us the entire way around the lake at nearly twenty-five mph. I sat on his wheel the entire time; I did not mind. The woman to my right on the Bone Ride was on a tri-bike and told me she had limited group riding experience. I asked her where she was from and she momentarily took her eyes off the road, looked at me, and touched wheels with the cyclist in front of her, making an all too familiar sound when wheels touch that often means a crash is imminent. I nervously moved to my left. She recovered nicely but noticed my anxiety and asked me if her riding made me anxious. I could not deny it and told her I was pleased no harm occurred.

Sixty miles into my first Bone Ride, the KS cycling team decided to drop to the back of the peloton and take a "natural break." Despite only drinking one cup of coffee, I saw this as my opportunity to relieve myself as well and be able to be brought back to the peloton without expending too much energy. I knew several young riders from the KS squad; they are good people. I was with two of them when I crashed and broke my clavicle for the third time. They tended to me well, so I felt a connection, but they are younger and faster than me. I reckoned that they would pull me back to the peloton without too much effort, but as I have often done, I overestimated my abilities. The peloton had moved significantly down the road by the time the break was finished; we could no longer see them. A sag wagon pulled up from behind and we drafted behind it at about thirty mph. I stayed with them for a while but begin to fall back and the moment I lost the draft I was done. I cannot sustain that pace without a significant draft.

One other KS rider fell back as well, so I rode with him. Graciously, Fast Freddy realized I was in trouble, got the attention of the sag driver, and told him to slow down. We caught the draft again and stayed with the sag wagon until arriving at the next town. The peloton was now in sight. The sag wagon stopped at a stop sign and the KS squad took off to retake the peloton. I hesitated too long at the stop sign and lost them again. I could see the peloton ahead riding over twenty mph and slowly made my way toward the comfort of the peloton. My progress was steady but slow and I was burning energy. Concerned that I was using too much energy, I began to question my choice of riding with KS knowing that I would pay for the effort later in the day. I looked down at my odometer and realized I had only gone fifty miles. One-hundred and ten more to go and my legs were already feeling the weight of the effort. Why was I so foolish to ride beyond my abilities? How much energy would I have to expend to catch the peloton? A voice interrupted my contemplation. "Are you all right?" asked the man driving the second sag wagon. A bit embarrassed, I responded, "Yes, but I got caught out at the last stop sign." They drove forward and I drafted behind the second sag wagon until I regained the peloton. Having rejoined the group, I vowed to be smarter in the remaining 110 miles, riding within my abilities, a vow I have made many times but seldom seem to keep, always getting caught up in the adrenaline rush of hanging on to a peloton clipping along at a fast pace.

I did not learn my lesson on my second Bone Ride. I told myself that I would not try to hang on to the lead peloton once it became a hammer fest on the way back to Wauwatosa. Instead, I would ride within myself and find a slower group to ride home with. As the speed ramped up outside Madison, I found myself in a good position, riding with my friend Jeremy and his brother-in-law Mark, both strong riders. I was fastened on Mark's wheel, feeling strong, when the lead group started up a hill and the pace increased. Here I was once again trying to keep up with the lead group. Mark could, but I could not. The gap between my wheel and his began to grow; he looked back and encouraged me. My lungs and heart were doing all they could, but to my surprise and confusion I could not hold the line. I looked around and realized I was all alone with more than sixty miles remaining, riding into strong headwinds by myself. I looked back in hopes that a slower group of riders that I might join was in sight, but I could not see anyone. My first thought was "this is going to be a very long day." Then I saw my friend Jeremy falling off the back of the peloton, and I did everything I could to catch up to him. "You did not need to wait for me," I said, albeit glad he did. "I didn't," he replied. "I couldn't hold the pace either." The two of us began to work together as we watched the peloton disappearing down the road. We worked together well; we had plenty of opportunity to do so the year we both rode 10,000 miles for the first time. We caught up with another ten riders who fell off the pace. They were a welcome sight, making our ride back to Wauwatosa much easier as twelve of us now shared the load.

BREAKING PROMISES

My third Bone Ride was my biggest success and failure. Not many Spokesmen had ridden the Bone Ride. It was primarily for racers. Cyclists who train for racing join clubs other than the Spokesmen. I have a competitive instinct that I'm not proud of. Perhaps it comes from my failures in basketball and running. Perhaps it is a desire to overachieve because of my small size. Whatever the psychological cause, I can get caught up in the moment and turn a friendly ride into a competition. I had convinced several Spokesmen to ride the Bone Ride with me and promised we could ride back together without the need to chase the fast riders back to Wauwatosa. I broke that promise. Coming out of Madison I could tell that three of the persons I planned to ride with were struggling. One was a fast racer who was on a steel frame because he cracked his carbon bicycle. He was also suffering from foot pain. He did not want anyone to wait on him; he usually stayed with the lead group easily. Another had stopped for a natural break on the way to Madison at a red light. The light changed and none of us realized he was not with us. He then got lost and rode the eighty-plus miles to Madison alone. He was exhausted. A third was not in the best shape that early in the spring. A moment of decision came when I had to choose to stay with the peloton or slow down with them as they began to drop off. I looked back and saw that they were struggling and decided to hang on to the wheel in front of me, uncertain that they were going to make it home. In fact, they did not but called one of their spouses to come and collect them. It was not my proudest moment. Something similar happened on my third RAW (Ride Across Wisconsin).

The 2019 RAW was the longest one-day ride I have done; 229 miles from La Crosse to Green Bay. Known as the "Driftless Region," La Crosse is on the border where Wisconsin, Minnesota, and Iowa come together. It is a beautiful area where the Ice Age glaciers left much of the area alone, yet valleys, rivers, and flat roads are surrounded by challenging bluffs and hills. The first sixty miles have considerable climbs until you arrive in central Wisconsin where the geography flattens out. RAW is sponsored by Wisconsin's Bike Federation; the professional Trek team leads out the event.

A group of Spokesmen had decided to ride together. I drove up to Green Bay with my friend Jim. He is from the area south of Green Bay and his family still operates a farm there. We took the back way and stopped at an excellent local diner. We met the other Spokesmen in Green Bay, hopped on a bus that took us across the state to La Crosse, and the next morning before dawn we began our ride together across the state. The pace was brisk with a slight tailwind. The line of riders with their red taillights blinking were strung out for what seemed to be more than a mile. It was difficult to keep track of everyone in the dark and a few of us got separated from the others. At the time, the few of us who were still together were uncertain if the others were behind or in front. Later we discovered one of them had a flat and had stopped to fix it. By the time we heard from them, we were a good eighty miles into the ride with a strong group of fifteen riders who were making excellent time. We chose not to wait for the others but to stay with our group. It was one of the strongest rides I have done, covering the 229 miles at 21.5 mph. I had ridden with a few friends I promised to ride with but had abandoned others. Cycling can bring out my worst instincts, generating vice as much as it does virtue. The ride matters, but friendship should matter more. Riding comes to an end; friendship is eternal. Thomas Aquinas defines the virtue of charity as friendship with God. Learning to be friends with others is preparation for the virtue of charity, which is the only of the three theological virtues, faith, hope and charity, that remains at the end.

5

Endings, Last Things

Every creature comes to its end. The end can be its mere finality or its purpose. If the brokenness of the middle is irredeemable, the end can only be a mere finality. It fades away without hope of being taken up into any purposeful existence. Evil, theologians and philosophers have argued, is like that. Rather than a being that persists, it is non-being dependent upon the fullness of being that alone can make possible non-being. There can be being without non-being, but there cannot be non-being without being, just as there can be truth without deceit, but not deceit without truth; good without evil, but not evil without good; and beauty without ugliness, but not ugliness without beauty. If there *were* no truth, goodness, or beauty, we would not be able to recognize deceit, evil, or ugliness. The world would lose its color and look the same as the homogenous gray on gray at twilight when we do not yet know if the sun is setting or rising. Nothing exists only at twilight. The rising of the sun brings not only light but also hope. G. K. Chesterton once wrote that the Creator is more like a child who finds each day full of promise than an adult who becomes jaded and easily bored. Any parent who has pushed a child on a swing knows what he means. Seldom does a child tire of being pushed. Instead, they cry out, "Do it again! Do it again!" The Creator is like that. Creation is not just some act at the beginning of time, but a constant event born out of divine eternity in which God says, "Let's do it again."

DESPITE IT ALL, LET'S DO IT AGAIN

For some reason, I never tire of cycling. Each ride is a new adventure, a way of engaging the goodness of existence through the power of self-movement. In the midst of the many unknowns in my life, cycling has been a consistent and constant companion. Along with daily commutes, regular weekday and weekend rides, special events, and the ride to California with Bob, I also went on two other lengthy bicycle trips, one with my roommate from Kenya around the inner circumference of Lake Michigan. That trip was cut short when our bicycles were stolen the day before completing our journey. We hitched a ride home. The other was with my brother Jeff, along the Blue Ridge Parkway, a gorgeous scenic route that did not seem to have a single mile of flat riding. He never took to cycling like I did, but that trip strengthened our friendship. We tell our children stories about it.

After the trip Bob and I made to California, cycling became a habit. I continued the journey by taking up bicycle commuting to work or school. Apart from one year in Honduras and the four years taking Amtrak between Chicago and Milwaukee, I have been a bicycle commuter since 1984. I view it as an extension of our cycling pilgrimage to California. Pilgrimage became a way of life; every bicycle ride repeats the joy of rendering the middle intelligible from the hoped-for end.

Hope, as the philosopher Terry Eagleton reminds us, is not optimism. The optimist merely looks on the "sunny side of life" while ignoring the conditions that make it possible. The optimist lacks sufficient reasons for their sense that everything will come out all right in the end. Neither nature nor politics lends much evidence for such a sentiment. Climate change may be too far down the road for us to do much about it. Even if we could agree on what should be done, the political will to do so is lacking and most likely will be until the consequences are unavoidable. The coronavirus pandemic has been something of a rehearsal for what we might face. If so, little reason for optimism exists. Secular and/or technological progress is more optimism than hope. At its best, it assumes that the present sufferings can be remedied by some future utopia that we are building on our own, as if the difficult life my grandmother had is somehow redeemed because her struggle and work made a better life for her children and grandchildren. But my comfortable life does not redeem her suffering. A socialist or capitalist future utopia will do nothing to comfort children miners crawling deep into the bowels of the earth to collect the minerals that we who are comfortable use in everyday life. What could redeem their suffering?

The theological virtue of hope is not optimism; it is born out of tragedy. The risen Christ bears the wounds of torture and execution for eternity.

No one passes into Sabbath rest without gazing upon those wounds. Yet those wounds were not the last word; death is defeated by life. If we do not look squarely at the hopelessness of death, then we cannot receive the gift of hope. It is from this lack of self-control, this recognition that we cannot secure our future that hope becomes necessary. One of my nieces asked me if I saw a light on the day my heart failed twice. I had to be honest. "No, there was only darkness that was driven out by the fear that accompanied waking and realizing that this could be the end." If there is hope, it is not something achievable by human power. We cannot overcome death; that end waits for each of us. Hope often arises not because we see a bright, shiny future, but because we see none at all. We have nothing remaining to do but to hope. Does this make the virtue of hope passive to its recipient? Perhaps, in part. Again Eagleton: "If there is a passive aspect to hope, its opposite in this respect is not so much despair as pure self-determination. What need is there for hope when one can be the author of oneself?"[16] It is this passivity, or better active receptivity, that requires a theological recalibration of the ancient virtue tradition. It lacks hope, and without hope there can be no faith. Faith and hope inevitably lead to charity.

A virtue is the actualization of a disposition that when actualized over time becomes second nature and creates the character out of which a person acts. Approaching the question of ethics from the perspective of virtue differs from approaching it through decisionist methods like that encapsulated by the trolley problem. Ethics becomes less about "what would you do if?" and more "who are you, how do you live in the world, and what do you consider to be a life well lived?" These two approaches certainly overlap, but the latter assumes the moral life is more about discovery than it is about performing actions from sources internal to a person. The thirteenth-century theologian Thomas Aquinas distinguished between sources internal and external to a person. Internal sources are capacities, or potentialities, a person already possesses. These capacities are not ethical until they become actualized into a second nature through habits. For instance, the desire to eat is a capacity that will need to be trained for one to live well, just as the potential for self-movement is exercised and formed through hiking, running, or cycling. Indulging every appetite or remaining sedentary leads to a poorly lived life.

External sources come from outside the person. Aquinas identifies grace as an external source, but he then raises the obvious question whether or not actions performed because of a source external to a person can be considered ethical. It seems appropriate to praise or blame someone for their exercise of internal capacities because they have some control over that exercise and can be held accountable. But if actions arise from external sources like grace, which for Thomas is the work of the Holy Spirit, then how could a person be responsible or accountable for their actions? They are beyond our control.

Having raised this question, Thomas turns to an unlikely source to explain how we can be ethical because of external sources: Aristotle's teaching on friendship. Good friendships make better actions possible than if we acted alone. Riding in a peloton makes for a nice analogy. In a peloton, one has the ability to ride effortlessly at speeds and distances one could never achieve on one's own. Friendship is like that. Friends guide us into forms of living well that we would neither achieve nor discover on our own. For instance, my friendship and subsequent marriage to Ricka led me, and continues to lead me, to engage in actions of hospitality and generosity that I otherwise might have neglected given the solitude that accompanies the life of the scholar. That friendship, like grace, is an external source prompting me in directions I might not otherwise go does not mean that it cannot also become an internal source. But I must follow a direction that I did not plan or anticipate for that to occur. In that sense, an ethical life of discovery is more like a pilgrimage. A pilgrimage begins in an act of faith. The pilgrim has reason to believe that the end will come about, but the end is imagined and not yet seen. The end is not chosen; it is set. The means to arrive at it are not set but vary and require deliberation and choice. A first step toward the end presumes faith. Hope then sustains each step along the way. In losing the practice of pilgrimage, we lose a practical way to receive through our actions the theological virtues.

LIFE AS A PILGRIMAGE

The Protestant Reformers objected to pilgrimages, associated as they were with relics and other practices that they considered to be superstitious. I consider that rejection mistaken, perhaps contributing to shifts in our understanding of time and space from an itinerary to a map, and from thinking of some times and spaces as more sacred than others to thinking of time and space as nothing but a quantifiable, regular, and secular reality. Along with the cycling pilgrimage to California, I have made three pilgrimages in northern Spain on the Camino Santiago de Compostela, known in English as the Way of St. James. It is a pilgrimage that goes back to the eleventh century, and one that granted pilgrims a plenary indulgence, a full pardon for one's sins. The Camino Santiago is not a single way; many starting points and different routes are possible. The most famous is the French Way that goes from St Jean Pied de Port to Santiago, a distance of 791 kilometers or

491 miles. It takes well over a month to hike that distance; I did not have the time to do the full French Way so I did approximately half that distance, on three different occasions.

My participation in the Camino came as a surprising gift. I knew about it because of the movie *The Way*, but I had no plans to do it. The Spanish department at Marquette University wanted to conduct a class that would hike the Camino and explore its many cultural and historical sites. The professor who desired to do this knew that she would have insufficient enrollment for a Spanish course alone, so she contacted the theology department to see if they had anyone who might be interested. Marquette students were required to do three theology courses at that time; if the course were team-taught and cross-listed the class would have sufficient numbers. Because my colleagues knew that I was in shape from cycling, they suggested that she ask me. She did and I thought it sounded like a marvelous opportunity. I began reading about the Camino, planning a course, and supplementing my cycling with hiking. Some people do the Camino with backpacks and others use a service that will ship your luggage from destination to destination. Our students insisted that we do it the right way by carrying everything with us, and so began the first of three pilgrimages that I made to the cathedral of St. James.

My Protestant forebears might not be pleased that I agreed to lead a group of pilgrims to the cathedral that legend suggests holds the bones of St. James. Pilgrims who arrive at the cathedral attend Mass, hoping to observe the famous Botafumeiro, a large thurible full of incense that is manually swung during worship. Then they line up to touch the statue of St. James to receive their indulgence. I'm still too Protestant to believe that a pilgrimage to a holy site merits an indulgence, let alone a plenary one. The pilgrimage does, however, require works that merit a good or holy life. For instance, it makes hope material and practical. Thomas Aquinas stated that the object of hope is something future that is difficult but possible to obtain. A pilgrim lives by hope in faith. In one sense, they have a vision of the end, arrival at the cathedral. In another sense, they can only see what is most immediate, the path lying before them. Each step contributes to obtaining the end; yet if pilgrims focus on one step alone, they would easily be tempted to despair. One or two feet is inconsequential when your goal is to travel more than 200 miles. The only way to travel that distance is to take a single step. In fact, a pilgrim can only take one step at a time. As inconsequential as each one is, they begin to accumulate until weeks later you take that final step into the cathedral and each step along the way is brought to its perfection. Each step makes possible the whole and the whole fulfills each step. Like the first step, the final step is but one step and yet that single step completes the others. Hope, the pilgrim discovers, requires patience and constancy.

The end of a pilgrimage is arrival at a destination, but more importantly it is the perfection of the person who undertakes it. People ask me if I had a spiritual experience during my pilgrimages and I must confess that I did not. The Camino is more arduous than I imagined. Day after day of hiking, working out pains in your feet, legs, hips, and back, never seeming to get sufficient food or drink, hardly lends itself to a spiritual experience. The Camino is bodily, but the body and the spirit are not opposed. It is in the fleshiness of the Camino, the overcoming of the inevitable physical pains, the gathering with other pilgrims from around the world for meals and wine, the pause to enjoy the beauty of the mountains that are also the cause of the pain, and the occasional isolation, that a pilgrim might realize what it means to be a creature in a vast landscape of creation. It is in learning to be a creature in all our fragility that a pilgrimage teaches about God and God's relation to creation. A pilgrimage is a daily reminder that whatever God is, you are not it, you have not yet found it, you are only on the way. You are a creature—contingent, fragile, dependent on others.

Pilgrims are confronted with two images of St. James along the Camino; one is the "Moor slayer," supposedly related to a vision of St. James that the Spanish army had when they were fighting the Moors in the eighth century. This disturbing image, enshrined in many churches along the way, reveals how a pilgrimage can be turned into a propaganda event to marshal the faithful for war. A Muslim student was on one of our pilgrimages and she was confronted by a less-than-charitable priest who told her, "Don't leave any bombs on the Camino." He was not joking. The other image of St. James is of a shepherd; it is an inviting, gentle image, more fitting with the hard reality of a pilgrimage. We stopped for worship one evening and two Franciscan priests held Mass, reminding us of these two images and encouraging us to seek the latter and flee the former. Their words gave us eyes to see our journey better. Had we not stepped into their chapel, we would have had a very different pilgrimage.

I made my first Camino in 2013. That next year my daughter Rebecca became engaged to Adam and they decided to prepare for marriage by hiking the Camino, which they did in 2014. I hiked it the following year in 2015, once again as part of a Marquette class. I had interviewed for the Maguire Chair in Ethics at Southern Methodist University earlier that spring and had not heard anything when we started the pilgrimage in late May. I had been asked to apply for the position the previous year and mentioned it to Ricka. She enjoyed her work as the oncology nurse manager at Froedtert Hospital and I was happy at Marquette, so we decided against it. The position was not filled, and I was asked again in 2015. Due to staff shortages, Ricka's workload had increased and had become overwhelming. She was working fifty to sixty hours per week. We anticipated that we would become grandparents over the next few years. Her work schedule would not allow her to spend the time with our children and grandchildren that she hoped for. With her encouragement, I applied and spent considerable time on my second Camino praying and contemplating whether I should return to the Methodists at SMU if the position were offered.

The second week on the pilgrimage, I received a text offering me the position. With only limited access to Wi-Fi, I let SMU know that I was on pilgrimage in Spain and would contact them when I returned to the states. I walked alone for several days deliberating about what to do. Our two daughters were close to us in Wisconsin. How could I move away from them now? Yet oddly enough, Ricka would have more opportunity to be with them because she would be able to retire. The Maguire chair provided options for me as a scholar that I never imagined possible. Moreover, there must have been some reason I had decided not to become Catholic after going through spiritual discernment. Perhaps it was time to return to the Methodists. By the time I arrived in Santiago, I was fairly confident that we would be moving to Texas.

Becky and Adam were married in 2015; their time on the Camino brought them closer together. A few years later they decided to hike it again and asked Ricka and me to join them. We received their invitation at the same time that Lindsey and Adam invited us to join them for a few weeks in Berlin. Adam's family came from Berlin; they had a furniture store in the city. As Jews, they saw the writing on the wall and fled Berlin in the middle of the night in 1936, only taking what they could carry with them. Adam's grandfather was eight years old. Because Germany has owned its past, it provides citizenship to family members of all survivors who fled the Nazis. Adam is a dual citizen, German and American. Our granddaughters Harper and Emma will be as well. We wanted to accept both invitations. Everyone arranged schedules so that we could, and we found ourselves in 2019 hiking the Camino followed by a trip to Berlin.

Ricka had a difficult time on the Camino. She prepared for it, but chronic arthritis in her feet made it almost unbearable. The second week, she found it nearly impossible to breathe when hiking up any incline. She would stop, catch her breath, and continue. She developed a cough that would not go away. Our second Sunday morning, we took her to a medical clinic to discover that she had a terrible case of bronchitis that was on its way to pneumonia. The doctor forbade her from walking. She took the next three days off, taxiing from place to place and waiting for us for the celebratory beer that marked each day's completed hike. After three days she felt better and was able to walk the final few days to Santiago.

Ricka and Steve arriving in Santiago at the Cathedral of St. James.

We then flew to Berlin, where we visited museums, parks, and historical sites, reconnecting with a past Adam only knew through his mother
and grandmother's stories. We walked silently through the Memorial to the
Murdered Jews of Europe, and went to the Topography of Terror, a museum
in a building that once housed the Gestapo and SS. This place of torture
had now become a site that showed the transformation ordinary citizens
went through to become the police who would terrorize their own people.

Each exhibit was another story of a farmer or worker or professional person caught up in horrendous evil. It all became too real, too close, and made you wonder if it could happen elsewhere. Police unaccountable to citizens is one of the gravest threats to freedom and democracy. A troubled but appropriate silence accompanied everyone as we went from exhibit to exhibit. I say "troubled" because it would be wrong to call it sacred; there was nothing sacred about that place.

Harper was fourteen months old and was walking and running with the ungainly movements of a toddler. She had found her voice, discovering its reverberation in the troubled silence of those haunted buildings. She fell and screamed, puncturing the silence. Recognizing the power of her voice, she would no longer be silent. At first I thought we needed to keep her quiet but then I found her loud interruptions appropriate. This child's very existence was an act of resistance against the horrendous evil the men and women in the exhibits' pictures represented. It was right that she was loud, crying and laughing. Perhaps it was not quite "the artistic taming of the horrible" because I'm unsure that villainous horror could be tamed, but it was a beautiful reminder that they did not have the last word. Harper's scream and laughter did. They were silenced; their power vanquished and their very lives examples of how not to live.

CONFRONTING THE CONDITIONS FOR EVERYDAY LIFE

Two weeks after my second Camino I found myself in Las Bambas, Peru as part of a global team of clergy and moral theologians doing a site visit in a copper mine run by a transnational corporation. MMG (Minerals and Materials Group) was founded in 2009 to "mine for progress." They knew that mineral mining had an unethical reputation throughout the world. Conflict mining secures many of the minerals that we use every day. People, often children, are forced to mine through the threat of violence; minerals are secured by war. Mineral mining has also been terrible for the environment, leaving places rich in minerals devastated from the environmental impact as the profit from those materials flows to wealthy investors and executives far from the area where the minerals are discovered. This global practice has led to the expression "the resource curse." Places rich in resources are some of the poorest, violent, and most undemocratic places in the world. Turn on a cell phone or open a computer, and the component parts most likely were made from minerals extracted under unethical conditions.

MMG is a corporation seeking to change the legacy of mining. Their mission is to "mine for progress" and they have a mission statement they requires mines to sign before they can be members.[17] In 2013, nineteen representatives from the mining industry convened for a "day of reflection" at the Vatican to discuss with the Pontifical Council for Justice and Peace how they could be held accountable for ethical mining practices.[18] They put together site visits by moral theologians from around the world in which external groups would visit mining sites, discuss their impact with workers, local leaders, clergy, and others impacted by the mine, and then gather with the mine executives for a day of reflection on which the groups of moral theologians would issue a report.

I had few expectations before the site visit to Las Bambas. Most of my previous experience with mining had occurred in the Appalachia region of the US. I was aware of the history of coal mining but had little knowledge of mineral mining in Peru and elsewhere. The village Ricka and I lived in in Honduras had been negatively impacted by a transnational shrimp and lobster corporation. That experience opened my eyes to the harsh reality that laborers could work for wages in a local economy producing a commodity for global export that they could not then afford even though it was a staple of everyday life. We buried children from malnutrition in a land rich with resources from shrimp and lobster that were mined for fast food restaurants in wealthy nations where people imbibed them for entertainment. Because of that experience, I have worked in the area of theological ethics and economics.

I entered into the mine site visit with suspicions. Would profit be more important than people? Would we be able to hear from, and see, the underside of mining? Would we primarily be engaging in propaganda for the mining industry? Although I had these suspicions, I agreed to participate because I knew several of the theological ethicists engaged in this project and trusted them. Moreover, the fact that the mining companies initiated the conversation and they had put together an ecumenical group of moral theologians from diverse countries and nationalities intrigued me. Moral theologians are seldom called upon these days to counsel anyone.

The site visit was fascinating. I learned about the complexity of the mining operation and its large scale. The Las Bambas mine was more than a work site; it was a small village of 18,000 people placed in a remote area that would forever change that place. The power of the grinder to reduce the mountain to rubble was impressive and alarming. The awareness by MMG about the environmental impact and the plans in place to restore the land to its original condition were reassuring. The village Fuerabamba had to be displaced in order for the mining operations to take place and we spent a great deal of time visiting and discussing the transition of that village to Nueva Fuerabamba made possible by the mining company. Clearly it sought to make the transition as ethical and sustainable as possible. It is still the case, of course, that mining requires the displacement of peoples and cultures and/or affects the surrounding areas in a variety of ways. For example, the neighboring town of Challhuahuacho exploded overnight, causing housing prices to rise and bringing with it new industries and problems.

The persons we spoke with were mixed about the impact of the mine on the village. Some saw it as progress and necessary for development. Others lamented the impact it had on their village. I was pleased that we were invited to speak with people holding a diversity of opinions without oversight from the mining executives. The local Catholic bishop offered a measured response. He acknowledged that the mine had brought order and stability to a region that did not have it before. He did not romanticize rural life before the mine, recalling how patriarchal and abusive it could be, but he also found the massive changes calling into question bonds of solidarity that unite people synchronically and diachronically. As something of an object lesson, he took us to a village some distance from the mining site that enabled us to compare (albeit briefly) the pace of life in the two areas.

I came away from this experience with more questions than answers. What struck me the most was the scope of the work and its inevitable impact on the area. The sheer size and money involved in the endeavor made the mining company the most powerful player in the area, more powerful than any local government. How will this kind of power relate to other forms such as the local, regional, and national political structures? What place is there for the church in this conversation? I was pleased that MMG initiated the conversation with the churches, and wondered how the church should respond. What is the role for other social bonds such as family, neighbors, villages, informal economies? What confronted me most was what a complex space all these overlapping social formations create.

A particular issue that was raised was the number of trucks that will be moving through the twenty-two villages that are on the road between the mine and the port. These are huge trucks carrying copper. Most of us would be alarmed to have them rolling continuously past our residence. How will this affect the lives of people who live along the road? What would it do to the commons that the road is? Minerals are necessary for everyday life. We cannot have them without mining. I came away from my experience at Las Bambas with a new appreciation for all who labor to make these everyday conditions possible and have continued to reflect on the theological and ethical significance of the things we take for granted, forgetting that they do not just appear but are produced by the toil of others. Little did I know that within five years from that day, mineral mining would affect my life in a profound way.

While recovering from my first pacemaker surgery, my cycling friend Josh sent me an NPR interview with Katherine E. Standefer on her book, *Lightning Flowers: My Journey to Uncover the Cost of Saving a Life*. Ms. Standefer is the same age as my oldest daughter and has a rare congenital cardiac condition known as "long QT syndrome." Although different from my condition, hers is also a problem with the electrical repolarization of the heart that causes syncope (passing out) and often requires placement of an ICD, an implantable cardioverter defibrillator. The ICD differs from my pacemaker in that it functions as both a pacemaker and a defibrillator. Because I never suffered from fibrillation, I did not need the defibrillator. When the cardiologist told me that I would not need it, I had no idea what that meant. I had never read up on pacemakers and ICDs. Since then, I have. The horror stories some persons have had with their defibrillator make me grateful that I do not need to worry about its potential to go off, medically warranted or not, and send its recipient into convulsive shocks. Standefer explains what it was like when hers went off for the first time: "my hands became claws. A maul cracked open my chest with a sickening thump, a hot whip tearing through my back."[19] The title for her exquisitely written work, *Lightning Flowers*, comes from the pattern made on the human body after a lightning strike. She wonders if the 2,000 volts that she suffered internally left its own mark inside of her body, one very present and yet unseen.

I had very little time to think about the social and economic conditions that make pacemaker technology possible on the day that mine was implanted. In fact, it was the furthest thing from my mind. As I previously mentioned, I knew the conditions that make much of our food possible. The memory of Juana's life is a constant reminder whenever I enter into a grocery store that the vegetables and fruit present there did not just miraculously appear. Work with chicken processing plants during my time in North Carolina put the lie to the idea of "boneless chicken." They must be deboned, and the conditions under which that takes place making for cheap chicken are indefensible. I used to give women a ride from the shrimp and lobster plant in Honduras to our evening worship service and listen to their stories of what it was like to work standing all day preparing shrimp and lobster for a global market. Once it was prepared, their wages were insufficient to purchase the product their own hands prepared. Standefer's *Lightning Flowers* brought my attention to the conditions that made possible the "saving" of my own life. She visited the mines that make the device preventing our heart failures, desiring, as she put it, that the extractive practices common to our modern life might be discovered "in nonexploitative and life-affirming ways that left communities and forests intact." She visited a mine cooperative in Kigali, Rwanda and interviewed workers. They seemed to be happy and worked in conflict-free mining, something that the Dodd-Frank Act of 2010 had taken up, requiring US companies on the New York Stock Exchange to disclose in their annual report so that consumers and investors would know where their minerals came from. Were we profiting from what amounted to modern-day practices of slavery? She found the Kigali cooperative promising with this proviso: "The story worked as long as we didn't compare the profits of corporations to what constituted a good living for the diggers."[20]

Standefer's work troubled me at many levels. At a personal level, it provoked me to such an anxious state that I had to put it down for a time. She had complications with her ICD that caused her to enter into the hospital for a possible extraction and replacement. I began reading her book after returning from a three-day hospital stay in Wisconsin confronting my own possible extraction and replacement after complications from my first pacemaker surgery.

My initial surgery had gone well. Within ten days I felt fine and even began easy indoor cycling. One month after surgery, Ricka and I drove from Dallas to Milwaukee to celebrate Thanksgiving with our children. We arrived in Milwaukee to seventy-degree temperatures in November. With the cardiologist's counsel, and Ricka's encouragement, I went out for a twenty-five-mile bicycle ride, circling a three-mile course next to our home so I would not be too far away if anything arose. I felt great; all was well. The next day I was sore and tired and the following day the incision site swelled and the skin around it became red and inflamed. At first, it was a small circle but the inflamed patch continued to grow, prompting alarm. Had I overdone it, causing some bruising? Was something else going on? Every cardiologist instructs new pacemaker patients that if there is swelling around the site, their doctor should be contacted immediately. One percent of pacemakers become infected after implantation; it is dangerous because the foreign material prevents antibiotics from clearing the infection and it can move into the bloodstream and heart, causing significant health risks. I sent pictures and an email to my cardiologist, who instructed me to go straight to the ER. The ER nurse outlined the red swollen skin with a marker to keep track of the progression of the infection. I was then admitted and put on IV antibiotics.

No one was certain what was occurring, but because I was presenting with a pacemaker infection, the doctors prepared for a possible surgery, prohibiting eating or drinking anything the next day. I was devastated, wondering how to find the emotional strength to go through this ordeal a second time, and this one would be worse because the first pacemaker had to be removed, the infection cleared, and then a second surgery undertaken to implant the new pacemaker. Once a pacemaker has been implanted, I discovered, it cannot be removed and reimplanted on the same side of the body. The new pacemaker would be implanted on the opposite side of my chest. The extraction surgery was explained to me early on the second morning in the hospital, but some uncertainty about my situation meant that the surgery had not yet been scheduled. Four cardiologists examined me at different times that day; one suggested that I would have the extraction surgery later in the afternoon. Finally, one came in whose specialty was extractions and said to me, "Although you are presenting as a pacemaker infection, the data do not indicate it." A pacemaker infection should be accompanied by a fever and an elevated white blood cell count; I had neither. He continued, "Our counsel is that we delay the extraction, finish the IV antibiotics, send you home for a lengthy treatment of antibiotics, and if your signs change then we will have you return to the hospital. We can always take a pacemaker out, but once we do we cannot undo what we have done." Ricka and I agreed that this was the wisest course and went home to finish the antibiotic treatment. Each day we would check to see if the swelling and redness diminished, which did not seem to be occurring. We waited anxiously to see if a fever developed.

Halfway through the antibiotic treatment, I had a follow-up visit with the cardiologist, who was still uncertain what was causing the infection. The swelling had not disappeared, but it had diminished. I was tired, even exhausted, but had no fever. He gave my chances at a second surgery at 30 percent, which was still concerning but not as depressing as the preparation for surgery that occurred in the hospital. One week later, the antibiotic course was finished, and I still had no fever. I had a follow-up visit and the cardiologist was pleased how the redness and swelling had dissipated. He did not think it was a pacemaker infection, but a cellulitis confined to the area around it. I thanked him for being cautious and following the data. One week after this visit, I came down with chills and a fever. This was alarming, but it was unaccompanied by any more swelling or redness at the incision, so the cardiologist thought it might be something else. I tested negative for coronavirus, but positive for pneumonia. I was placed back on antibiotics and found myself for the third time since the initial cardiac incident confined to bed. The antibiotics worked; my lungs cleared.

Once the pneumonia departed, the redness and swelling returned. I still showed no symptoms of an infection in my bloodstream or heart, had no fever, nor an elevated white blood cell count, but after fighting the infection for two months the infection was clearly winning and I was tired of feeling poorly. I sent pictures of the red, angry incision site to my cardiologist. The incision had now reopened and the team asked me to come in. They looked at it and the cardiologist told me the words that I did not want to hear: "We are going to have to extract it, let the incision clear for a few days and implant another pacemaker on the other side of your chest." At first, I was devastated. I had gone through so much the past three months and now I had to do it again. But I was also exhausted by the soreness and discomfort at the pacemaker site. After four treatments of antibiotics, one occurring intravenously for three days in the hospital, I was ready to try something new. Originally, they planned for an extraction followed by a three-day hospital stay on antibiotics and then reimplantation. What worried me most was that I would be without a pacemaker between the extraction and reimplanation. I had visions of what happened that fateful day in October when my heart failed. Would I be living through that again? I did not want my heart to spiral down causing another episode. My pacemaker had only been pacing the heart 1 to 6 percent of the time, so the cardiologist thought that I would not need a temporary pacemaker and that given the infection, the risk of a temporary one was too great. I would be carefully monitored in the cardiac unit with defibrillator pads that could shock my heart back to its normal rhythm if it acted up, or perhaps better put, down.

When I arrived for the pacemaker extraction, the cardiology team decided at the last moment that it would be best to change the plan. No one was certain what was causing this strange, persistent infection and a few days between the extraction and reimplantation would be insufficient to culture the site and let the infection clear. "We would like to send you home on an antibiotic treatment for two weeks with a 24/7 monitor and do the reimplantation once the infection has cleared." The words produced panic. I would now be without the pacemaker for more than two weeks rather than three days, and rather than having the comfort of being in the hospital, I would be at home. I looked at Ricka and saw a similar reaction on her face. My first thought was that extracting the pacemaker and living without it for several weeks would return my health to its previous weakened state. Ricka thought the same and asked, "What do I do if he has another complete heart block?" The cardiologist said, "Give him two chest compressions and he will come back." Although meant to be reassuring, this intensified the panic. "He will have a monitor that sends a signal to first responders if anything goes wrong." We were still not comforted. Yet after hearing the risks involved in a too-quick reimplantation, we agreed that this was the best course of action.

The first few days at home on the monitor were anxious because we did not know what to expect. I was told to be a couch potato and avoid any exertion. Ricka would not let me out of her sight. I rose early, often before 5

AM, and read in a sunroom on the main floor of our home. I did not ask her to adopt my schedule, but Ricka would get up when I did, follow me down the stairs, and sleep on the couch in the next room so she could hear if I became distressed. During the day, whenever I became too quiet, she would yell out, "You all right?" Despite the anxiousness of those first few days, to be loved so well, deeply, and tenderly filled me with joy. It also showed us that the radical instability of my heart during that fateful weekend in October was not an inevitable aspect of everyday life. I had a few minor episodes waiting for the infection to clear, but nothing like what occurred in October. My heart condition would come and go; there would be spells of sickness but also wellness. I still needed the pacemaker and dare not drive, ride a bike, or engage in much of anything where I could hurt myself or others for fear of losing consciousness. For three weeks, we had an isolated, sedentary lifestyle waiting for the infection to clear in anticipation of the second surgery. The lab reports indicated the pacemaker was infected but it had not progressed into the bloodstream or the heart. Despite the ordeal, it was good and necessary that it was extracted. On February 10, four months after my first pacemaker, I received my second.

Standefer's book arrived during my first at-home antibiotic treatment, when the question whether I would need the second surgery was not yet settled. Her vivid prose detailing how the sense of having foreign materials in your body keeping you alive never goes away; how the pacemaker will keep working even after you are dead and will need to be extracted by your undertaker; how every time you are sick you worry that it might be the pacemaker; how another surgery always hangs over you given the limited battery life of the device—undid me. I am seldom an anxious person, but a wave of anxiety swept over me as the reality of my changed situation hit home in a way that I had previously not contemplated. Life had drastically changed. Even if I could return to my previous practices, I could not imagine that they would ever seem normal again. The foreign metals were here to say.

A second question her book confronted me with was the privilege that I had to receive not only one but two pacemakers, the first within the time it had taken to ride a century the day before and the second after being seen by a team of cardiologists. This freedom places me in a privileged minority both in the US and globally. Standefer's desire to know the conditions that saved her life raised troubling questions about the political and economic contexts that allow some people to enjoy technological progress unavailable to others. In 2019 on the African continent, where many of the materials for ICDs and pacemakers come from, five countries did not have a single cardiologist. Whereas 300 to 1,200 persons in the US, Canada, and Europe per million have these implantable devices, it is only one to seven persons per million in Africa.[21] The freedom my pacemaker potentially gives me for a longer life to watch my grandchildren grow is not available to many persons throughout the world with similar needs.

Standefer lacked health insurance when her need for a device arose. She had to move to a different state and seek residency there to be eligible for a treatment that I received by showing up at the closest hospital, not even inquiring if they were in network. Were it not for the Affordable Care Act, she would not have been able to afford the life-saving device. Trump's election, and the prospect that the ACA would be overturned, held implications for her health that I did not face. As a university professor, I had excellent health insurance. My son lacked insurance for a brief time while teaching music at a nonprofit school until he could get on the exchange. I thought about what it would mean for us if he needed the medical treatment that I did.

I had a health savings account that included a high deductible, but one that I could afford with the HSA. I gave little thought to whether or not I could afford what I needed to sustain my life. Of course, I discovered that even with top quality health insurance, there were costs upon costs that continued to roll in. I easily met my deductible, but it did not include "out of pocket expenses," which could be up to $10,000. When I received my first $2,500 expense for the ER visit, I called the insurance company and asked why I had to pay such a large amount since I already met my deductible. They informed me that ER doctors are seldom in network and thus I was required to pay this amount because it was neither met by the deductible nor the "out of pocket expenses" but fell under a third category, "out of network expenses," that could be up to $20,000. The first hour-long conversation with the insurance company was unsatisfying; I was told I had to meet the expense. I called a few days later and spoke with a helpful person who said that because it was a life-or-death situation the insurance company would treat it as an in-network expense. Even with excellent insurance, billing remains mysterious. Months past my first hospital visit, bills continue to trickle in, and I remain confused as to what I should or should not pay. The second surgery occurred two weeks into the new year in which I had to meet the deductible again before insurance kicked in. The entire ordeal cost us more than $8,000 out of pocket, but we could afford it. Standefer faced much worse than I did. She rightly states, "The system is not built to deliver care. It is built to maximize profit."[22] Not everyone is free to receive the care that I did.

FREEDOM FOR CARE

Cycling, as I mentioned above, gave me the freedom of self-movement that I have enjoyed within and outside the US. Freedom, however, is not something that exists without the political and social conditions that make it possible. If the few angry motorists who would like to ban cyclists from the roads would have their way, the freedom of self-movement could be severely restricted. The pandemic has raised acute questions about freedom, health, and economics. When should we open businesses, schools, houses of worship, etc.? How should they be opened and who decides? These questions are complex, and I make no attempt to resolve them, but I fear that the way Americans think about freedom and markets prevents sound ethical reasoning about such questions. To put it bluntly, the "free market" has become an idol to which we are willing to make sacrifices. It has not "freed" many for the health care that they desperately need. The lives of those most susceptible to COVID-19, the elderly, the infirmed, low-wage "essential" workers, are offered to insure that the Dow increase. As the economist Paul Krugman asked in a *New York Times* column, "How many will die for the Dow?" A society that sacrifices people on the edges of society for stock prices is a society that needs to think again about ethics.

We should begin that rethinking with what ought to be a noncontroversial statement: markets are not free—never have been, never will be. They are not natural living things. They have no will, no intellect, no agency of their own. Markets are artificial human constructs. When someone refers to the "free market," they have not yet said anything concrete, practical, or meaningful. Good ethical reasoning will begin with this basic principle: people are free or unfree and markets should serve the freedom of people. Markets that make people free are good; markets that work at the expense of human life are wicked. This should be the most important principle for relating health and economics. For it to work properly, we must have some idea of what it means to be a free human being.

Philosophers divide freedom between negative and positive accounts. Negative freedom is freedom *from*. It is further divided in terms of a libertarian or liberal freedom—freedom as non-interference—and a republican freedom—freedom as non-domination. Positive freedom is freedom *for*. To be free is not merely a lack of constraint, as important as that is, but also to have one's life oriented toward what is good and true, to what makes life worth living, toward a proper end. Positive freedom assumes such an end. We choose the means to the end, but as with a pilgrimage, we cannot choose the end. The end is given, discovered, intrinsic to God's good creating action.

These views of freedom are not necessarily opposed. To be free *for* something involves not being interfered with in pursuit of human flourishing, nor dominated by others inhibiting that pursuit. The positive account of freedom is usually associated with ancient ethical thought and Christian ethics. The negative account is more modern. It tries to make life together possible under the pluralistic and often competing accounts of good and truth that define modern society. The negative accounts arise from the assumption that we cannot find agreement about what is true and good so that our life could be ordered to it; there is nothing to be discovered, no end except that which we choose for ourselves. Thus, we abandon the quest to discover it and accept negative freedom alone. No one gets to interfere with another's pursuit of goodness or understanding of truth. Yet the coronavirus exposed the limits to this negative account. We need to know the truth about the pandemic, and have it publicly explained in a compelling and accessible way. We then need to figure out what good or goods, what ends, should be served given the truth of our reality. Unfortunately, even the pandemic has become a casualty of our incessant culture warring, so that we are unable to make reasonable judgments based on what is true, to the best of our knowledge, rather than assuming that every claim for truth is a veiled play for power. Negative freedom cannot move us beyond this impasse. We need something more, something positive, and here is where people of faith can assist.

Most people of faith, I would submit, affirm a positive account of freedom. Take this petition from the United Methodist Church's prayer of confession: "Free us for joyful obedience." It is by no means unique to Methodism, but readily found in other traditions as well. The crucial term is "for." Freedom is positive; it is *for* something. Similarly, the motto of Southern Methodist University, where I teach, is *Veritas liberabit vos*—"the truth will set you free" (John 8:32). Freedom is joyful obedience to accomplish the good intrinsic to God's creating, sustaining, and redeeming of human life. Freedom is to know and live from what is true. Freedom is not the ability to assert one's power separate from this goodness and truth. To ignore the truth and neglect the good is the road to serfdom. It is to be ruled by false powers like the illusory "free market" that no one has ever seen because it does not exist.

A positive account of freedom entails that we are free *for*, and not *from*, each other. Our lives are implicated in each other's. Because markets are artificial constructs, they are always regulated in myriad ways. The question is never whether they are regulated, but who is served by what regulations. This is the question that we must ask, a question that libertarian freedom fails to pose. For instance, to force meat-packing workers to work because they are essential workers at the expense of their health is a severe regulation on their lives, and a form of serfdom. That a few can direct the labor of others without their consent, or without viable options, lets us know that we are not yet free for each other. That we preserve a so-called free market at the expense of human lives thumbs our nose at the goodness of creation and offends its Creator. We can do better, but not so long as we bow the knee to a nonexistent entity, a "free" market, and assume that it must be preserved at all costs. Marketing health for profit restricts freedom, making health available only to the privileged.

THE HEART OF THE MATTER

Life-enhancing medical devices have always been with me. I began life with one. Born with clubfeet, I required a Dennis Brown Splint for the first year of my life. It is two shoes connected with a metal bar that forces your feet into a normal position. I learned to crawl with it. My parents told me that I beat my crib to pulp with it. Metal prepared me for life and now metal sustains it. I will end my life with a pacemaker that keeps beating when my heart decides, against my wishes, to slow down and keep slowing down until it stops. Everything happened so quickly on October 11 that I had no time to reflect upon it. Clammy, uncomfortable, with an irregular heartbeat, I lay on the couch doing what scholars do, weighing my options, thinking about next steps. I opened my computer to research best cardiac hospitals when Ricka with her practical wisdom intervened and said, "Let's get to the nearest hospital." By noon that day the lifesaving metal device was in me. Its finality came first, reflection came after.

Living through that experience has prompted much reflection. A little more than one month out, I went for a walk with my children and they noticed that I was unusually quiet. They expressed concern. I responded, "Have you noticed I'm in a reflective mood?" It became something of a running line for a few days: "Have you noticed Dad is in a reflective mood?" Why? What? What if? What next? Such questions preoccupied space in my head. Books on heart disease, pacemakers, living and dying overtook my planned reading on the medieval theologians Ghazali, Anselm, and Maimonides.

Much as something sinister seemed to seize my breath and stop my heart, something providential, or at least fortuitous, restored it. Had I experienced heart failure in our first year of marriage in Honduras where no cardiac health care was available, would it not have been different? What if it had occurred with Bob cycling in the remote desert in Utah, or while much later hiking on the Camino, distant from any town? What if it took place in Buffalo, Indiana, a good hour's drive from a hospital with cardiac care? What if I were alone in Dallas and Ricka had not yet returned? What if I did not have health insurance and took the time to count the cost/benefit ratio of staying alive? The conditions could have been different producing a different outcome. Were they providential or fortuitous?

Whether the events of October 11 are described as providential or fortuitous has significant implications. If I claim providence restored my heart that day, then what do I do with all those for whom the conditions for restoration of health differed, for those who did not have access to health care? Did providence abandon them, willing something other than life? Such a claim could easily divide humanity into the damned and elect by some arbitrary decree, overlooking the access to wealth and medical care that are significant reasons my fate differed from others. Justice demands some other way of telling my story that avoids easy appeals to providence, as if I'm the elect and do not need to face the conditions that make my life possible. But if I altogether neglect providence and tell the story as mere good fortune, as only contingent circumstance, then do I not tacitly call into question the prayers prayed on my behalf and the action of God in the world? Is it not a subtle atheism that renders God inoperable in human affairs for the sake of justice as fairness that refuses to consider divine action altogether? God is excluded from consideration because the inequities that make possible my access to a pacemaker, access that comes from deplorable economic conditions of mining materials, appear unjustifiable if God exists. Better not to think of God at all than think of a God who arbitrarily conveys life and death, redeeming some and damning others.

If I cannot sing the Wesleyan hymn—"Come sinners to the Gospel feast, Let every soul be Jesus' guest, You need not one be left behind, For God hath bid all humankind"—then I could not bow the knee to God. Better to stand on the side with Satan in Milton's *Paradise Lost,* who refused to bow and encouraged others to do the same. Yet, Satan does not see clearly. Excluding God from consideration does nothing to affect or alter our deep inequity. It is still there. We simply feel better about it because God is not responsible and now the ability to change it resides solely with us. That should provide little comfort. At most it makes us optimistic; it gives little hope. Is there another way to think about divine action, inequality, and justice?

If I will my life by affirming the conditions of inequity that make it possible, then I am immoral, less than human, willing to damn the masses solely for the sake of my longevity. I did not need the reality of a pacemaker living inside of me to know that. The shrimp factory in Honduras made it obvious, but I should have recognized it earlier in my grandmother's life. Yet, if I lack gratitude for the life restored to me, then that too would be less than human, as if I should not have been thinking about holding my grand-daughters again and instead fixated on the injustices that make my life, any life, possible on the day my heart failed. The latter sentiment can end in a celebration of death where everything is finally fair. Every human being rots at the end and all the inequity in the world cannot change that fact—yes, this too is God's justice. But God is, as Gustavo Gutiérrez beautifully put it, a God of life and not a God of death.

Death should only be understood as a judgment that makes possible conditions for new life; it is not the answer to life. I remain grateful for life restored and must do so without willing the inequitable conditions that make it possible. To will the latter with the former is to will death for others that I might live. To refuse gratitude for life because of the unequal conditions that make every life possible seems ever so subtly to will the death of all for the sake of justice. Perhaps this is why some philosophers of justice become anti-natalists, considering it an unjust act to bring children into the world? Affirming their own existence, they deny it for others. Do not be afraid. They are a distinct minority who will pass away. Providence did not abandon my uncles when they died in their fifties nor my grandmother when a stroke took away her ability to speak in her early seventies. Providence is not only about life as longevity, as if it could be quantitatively measured. That way lies death. Had I died at sixty my life would still have been beautiful, and I would have willed it all over again. Every heart eventually fails; I have the blessing of being made more aware than many of that reality.

The heart is the strongest muscle in the body, pumping oxygenated life through its arteries and then returning by its veins to the heart through a circulatory system that works on average 100,000 times per day. All that work goes unnoticed unless someone sits quietly and intentionally listens for it or overworks it and feels its intense activity. When it quits working, when it completely rests, I can attest, you no longer notice it. You notice it slowly failing, but when it fails you slip into darkness and only notice what occurred if its beating returns.

The muscular heart with its repetitive circulatory system is fired by a complex electrical system whose measurement was first discovered by scientists at the same time the bicycle was invented. Since then, we have come to learn a great deal about that electrical system. Cells in the heart depolarize and then polarize, releasing electrical charges that create a circuit within the heart starting in the sinoatrial (SA) node that is in the upper right of the heart and generating the heart's "sinus rhythm." Like a harmonious symphony, this rhythm assumes the proportionate cadence and cooperation of the atrioventricular (AV) node that call forth a response from the electrical system known as the "His-Purkinje network," prompting the muscles to contract and force the blood through the body. The heart is a circuit within a circuit. An electrical current that goes in a circular motion within the heart makes sure that blood goes round and round the body, making forward movement possible. This movement is not eternal; the circuits and the forward movement come to their end. Yet it is circular motion that allows forward progress.

Some of the cells that make up this circuit are called pacemaker cells. They pace the heart's electrical circuitry, insuring the movement. A time gap exists between the SA node and the AV node. The artificial pacemaker implanted in the chest contains wires that work with or in place of these nodes. They can be set by a technician to insure that the heart only beats so fast or that it continues to beat when it goes too slow. The time gap between the SA and AV nodes can also be set. My pacemaker was first set at sixty bpm, which was too high, and it was pacing my heart 60 percent of the time. The cardiologist then set it to fifty bpm and it only paced it 1 to 6 percent. I felt much better after that. Once the cardiologist realized that I did better at fifty bpm, he also extended the time gap between my SA and AV node, giving my heart the chance to do the work before the pacemaker did its. This not only helps my heart continue working and strengthening the muscle, but it also extends the pacemaker's battery, which can last from eight to ten years.

A pacemaker requires periodic service. With my earlier St. Jude device, a circular magnet was placed around it connected to a computer and the algorithms played with to get the right settings. I now have a Medtronic that contains Bluetooth. The technician only needs to come close to my heart to check it. To make sure the pacemaker is working properly, the technician first speeds it up and patients sense their heart rate elevating as it would under stress or a rush of adrenaline. Then they slow it down. These moments mark the acute realization that your circuitry has been commanded by artificial means. You have lost control of your heart. It is unnerving, but is it not true of everyone? The heart cannot be commanded by autonomous action. It is there, doing its work internally but almost like an external source.

My cardiac situation is unlike most "athlete's hearts." When they heard about my incident, several cycling friends encouraged me to read *The Haywire Heart: How Too Much Exercise Can Kill You, and What You Can Do to Protect Your Heart*. Written by long-distance athletes, one of whom is a cardiologist and one, Lennard Zinn, who suffered a cardiac episode in his fifties, it is a must read for anyone intending to run or cycle throughout their life. I read it in one weekend, trying to understand what had occurred to me and how I might have contributed to it. It is a mixture of the science behind the heart and stories of athletes that had experiences similar to mine. Most stories relate cardiac episodes like Zinn's; during a strenuous exertion the heart takes off, jumping from a normal high rhythm to a dangerously high one, usually well over 200 bpm. The heart induces fibrillation, where it begins to quiver or beat chaotically. Most cardiac incidents for long-distance athletes result in a too-fast heartbeat known as tachycardia and require an implanted cardio device that includes a defibrillator. Mine was the opposite. I suffered from bradycardia, a too-slow heartbeat. The average heartbeat is between sixty and 100 beats per minute. During strenuous exercise, it can increase anywhere from 140 to 180. I never experienced problems with too high a heart rate. My abnormality only occurred when my heart began to rest. My regular heart rate was between fifty and sixty bpm, but I developed a condition in which my heart would start to rest, slow down, and continue slowing down until it came to rest at dangerously low rates, including the two occasions where it rested altogether by stopping.

A certain irony accompanies my unique situation as a theologian whose problem is that his heart rests too much. In Jewish and Christian theology, God rests on the seventh day of creation and all of creation should reflect that rest. As the third commandment states:

> Remember the Sabbath day, and keep it holy. Six days you shall labor and do all your work. But the seventh day is a Sabbath to the Lord your God; you shall not do any work—you, your son or your daughter, your male or female slave, your livestock, or the alien resident in your towns. For in six days the Lord made heaven and earth, the sea and all that is in them, but rested the seventh day; therefore the Lord blessed the Sabbath day and consecrated it. (Exodus 20:8–11)

The Sabbath is a day of rest, but the cycle of resting on the seventh day is not limited to temporal existence; eternity itself, the "last things" prepared for creatures, is to rest in God's rest. The purpose of life is to enjoy God's rest, a Sabbath in which everything rests from its labors and lives from divine abundance. Rest is the Jubilee Year when slaves are set free, workers no longer labor, refugees are returned to their homes, and everyone has not only a sufficiency of life but its abundance.

Labor, especially arduous labor, is for Christian theology not something to be celebrated. It does not give people their dignity; being created in the image of God provides that. Arduous labor is a sign that things are broken. We should hope for its cessation just as we pray, "Thy kingdom come, thy will be done, on earth as it is in heaven." Rest gives things their purpose. This rest is not boredom or monotony, but like the circular motion that constitutes the body it is an intensity of motion that reflects the triune God, in whose image we are made. God is a circular motion of such intensity among three persons that God is motion without movement, an eternal coming from and going toward that occurs without any temporal passage from an origin to its termination. God is pure act within whom true rest is possible. It is why the appropriate Christian response to death is, "May they rest in peace and rise in glory."

I have pronounced those words over others many times. I am in no hurry to have them pronounced over me, but the events since October 11 have made that inevitability seem more practical than theoretical. My years of cycling, and the last five or so years reflecting on those years of cycling, have taught me much about myself, about God's good creation, and about the fragility and goodness of being a creature. I am not optimistic, but I cannot but be filled with hope, enough hope to want to say, "Let's do it again."

Endnotes

1. See Cynthia Carr, *Our Town: A Brutal Lynching, a Haunted Town, and the Hidden History of White America* (New York: Three Rivers, 2007).

2. James Baldwin, *The Fire Next Time* (New York: Vintage International, 1991), 25.

3. Carr, *Our Town*, 128.

4. Carr, *Our Town*, 128.

5. James Cameron, *A Time of Terror: A Survivor's Story* (Milwaukee: Life Writes, 2015), 93–95. Cynthia Carr is an investigative journalist whose grandfather lived in Marion during this time and was a member of the Klan. Her *Our Town* investigates Cameron's telling of the story, offering details that slightly revise or better supplement his personal account.

6. The editorial, "In need of a pope? Protestants and the papacy" can be found here: https://www.christiancentury.org/article/2005-05/need-pope.

7. Long, "My Church Loyalties: Why I Am Not (Yet) Catholic." https://www.christiancentury.org/article/2014-07/my-church-loyalties.

8. At Michael's suggestion, I participated in the beginning and early development of the Ekklesia Project, which intends to be an place for ecumenical friendships. More information can be found here: http://www.ekklesiaproject.org.

9. See Robert Song's *Covenant and Calling: Towards a Theology of Same-Sex Relationships* (London: SCM, 2014) for a good discussion of these passages.

10. http://sites.rootsweb.com/~ialqm/White%27sInstitute.html.

11. James Longhurst, *Bike Battles: A History of Sharing the American Road* (Seattle: University of Washington Press, 2015), 240.

12. Longhurst, *Bike Battles*, 16.

13. Longhurst *Bike Battles*, 54–57, 60, 80–82.

14. *New York Times*, "This Los Angeles Team Wants to Diversify Cycling," December 1, 2020.

15. https://www.bicycling.com/news/a20004637/the-bone-ride/.

16. Terry Eagleton, *Hope without Optimism* (New Haven, CT: Yale University Press, 2017), 69.

17. The vision and values statement can be found here: https://www.mmg.com/who-we-are/our-vision-and-values/.

18. See chapter 5 of Esther Reed's *The Limits of Responsibility: Dietrich Bonhoeffer's Ethics For a Globalizing Era* (New York: T. & T. Clark, 2018) for a discussion of how this

came about. My own participation in the site visit to Las Bambas was due to Dr. Reed's invitation.

19. Katherine E. Standefer, *Lightning Flowers: My Journey to Uncover the Cost of Saving a Life* (New York: Little, Brown Spark, 2020), 1.

20. Standefer, *Lightning Flowers*, 197–202.

21. Standefer, *Lightning Flowers*, 153.

22. Standefer, *Lightning Flowers*, 223.

CPSIA information can be obtained
at www.ICGtesting.com
Printed in the USA
BVHW031941011221
623024BV00005B/284